GET READY!

GET READY!

Practical Ideas to Prepare

You for Ministry

Karen Porter

Get Ready!
ISBN-978-0-9853563-0-9

Bold Vision Books LLC
PO Box 2011
Friendswood, Texas 77549

Table of Contents

Get Ready!

Introduction

What an awesome privilege to follow God's call! Has He called you to teach His Word, to speak to groups about spiritual matters, to write His message in books and magazines, or to serve His cause in your community or church? If you have determined to follow Him, you have started the path to amazing blessings because those who serve, speak, teach, and write learn more in the behind-the-scenes preparation than those who are listening to you speak or who read what you write.

You are traveling a remarkable journey whether you are a seasoned Christ-follower or a newbie just getting started. Only God could put the thought in your head and heart to serve, teach, speak, or write, and He will be with you all the way. Your job is to thoroughly prepare and be ready for whatever He has in mind for you.

GET READY! is about spiritual growth—how you and I can be changed by the grace and mercy of God.

But too often, we have the wrong idea about spiritual growth. We think it is about a formula. In fact, most of us would like spiritual growth to be the result of a formula. Read x number of verses, pray x number of hours, learn Hebrew, memorize some important passages, and be able to name the top ten doctrines. The formula equals a spiritually deep speaker or writer.

A formula like that would fit right into our modern world, wouldn't it? We could follow the formula and pick up our black belt in spiritual growth in a few months. But spiritual growth isn't a system or program or even a path to follow. Sure, prayer, Bible study, communion, and other disciplines will help you grow, but these are procedures and techniques not growth.

In his book *Messy Spirituality,* author Michael Yaconelli says spiritual growth *begins with desire, not guilt; passion, not principles; desperation, not obligation;* and growth happens when we travel the *road of failure, frustration, and surprise.*

God doesn't call us to be perfect in the spiritual disciplines, but He does call us to want to be with Him and to want to learn about Him and to want to hear His voice in the middle of our frantic lifestyles and disappointments, catastrophes, and failures.

This book will give you tools to find Him in your daily pursuit of spiritual growth, and these tools will help you capture what you learn so that you can use it when you write or speak or teach.

Paul wrote these words in 1 Corinthians 16:9, "For a wide door for effective work has opened to me." God has opened a door in front of you, too. It is a wide door ready for you to enter and just on the other side, is His calling to you. It is effective and fulfilling work. I'm praying you will open the door and move forward.

I'm glad that you've chosen to read *GET READY!* and I'd love to hear from you. Write me at kaeporter@gmail.com.

10

LIVING ON GOD'S HOLY HILL

CHAPTER 1

To spend little time with Jesus is to accomplish little for Him.

*"What we do for the Lord is entirely dependent upon what
we are in the Lord. Further, what we are in the
Lord wholly depends upon what we receive from the Lord.
And what we receive from the Lord is directly
proportional to the time we spend alone with the Lord in prayer."* [1]

PLAYING THE "E" GAME

Do you like to play games? I do. We play a lot of them at our house. If we don't have one handy, we make one up. Sometimes the made-up games are the most fun. We not only like to play, we play to win. My husband gets cranky if I win and then with great fanfare announces that this particular game is suddenly unscriptural and forbidden. He doesn't like to lose.

One game we play is called the "E" game, also called "Who's going to put gas in the car?" I try to be sure the gas gauge will hit empty just when I know George is going to get into the car. Then he must fill the tank, and I win the game. Sometimes, I'll drive on fumes just to win.

One week the gas gauge began creeping down toward the "E" mark on Monday. The next day, a small box on the dashboard read "low gas." But I knew that George would be driving the car on Wednesday evening, so I waited.

Wednesday morning, a small, lighted gas pump appeared in the window—the third reminder that the car needed gas.

Wednesday afternoon, a sign on the dashboard started flashing the word "low." My fourth reminder. But he was about to drive, so I waited.

When I reached home, George was deep into a project—surrounded by stacks of books. He cancelled his plans for the evening, so I had to drive alone. Not long after I climbed into the car, a bell started ring, ding, dinging. I pushed the accelerator, and the car sputtered to a stop.

Yes, I had ignored all the indicators in my car. The gauge moving into the red danger zone. The square showing low fuel. The image of a gas pump in the window. The word "low" blinking on and off on the front panel. Even the ringing bell.

Spiritually, we play the game too. We exist a long time without refueling. We ignore all the danger signals. We think all is well— as we depend on our spiritual fuel tanks. We pretend to everyone, even those closest to us, that all is well. But sooner or later, we run out of fuel, and our spirits sputter.

Our fuel is low because we don't spend time with God. Being alone with God creates a partnership that allows us to participate in His work. Accepting Christ as your Savior puts you into a relationship with God. You are His child and all God has is potentially yours. But spending time with God develops a fellowship with Him, which means we actually draw upon all those resources.

Relationship is us possessing God. Fellowship is God possessing us. Fellowship with God is the key to vital Christianity. And you will only develop true fellowship if you spend time with Him.

Without fellowship, relationship suffers and we start a downward spiral toward isolation from God. The spiral begins when we stop reading the Bible. Then we don't feel like praying and our worship becomes lifeless and uninteresting. That's when a critical mindset moves into our hearts. Isolation follows a critical heart.

No Bible Reading

> Empty Prayers
>> Dull Worship
>>> Critical Heart
>>>> Isolation

Isolation's darkness begins with the first small step of shutting out the light of God's Word. What surprises me is how fast this downward progression to darkness can happen. If I fail to spend time with God one morning, by three in the afternoon I am criticizing everything and everyone. About that time, the family gets home from work and school. Arguments, harsh words, short tempers surface. Each family member is suddenly isolated from the rest and the whole family is isolated from God. We slid down the spiral in one day.

ADAM AND EVE

Adam and Eve lived in a perfect environment. Beautiful trees and plants filled the garden. I can imagine colorful flowers, flowing brooks, and butterflies. It was never too hot. Never too cold. Perfect. Food grew in abundance. Boredom never set in. They had everything —a wonderful relationship with each other.

He had a perfect wife. She had a perfect husband. Yet perfection couldn't satisfy them completely. They needed to spend time with God every day. *God came to them in the cool of the evening* (Genesis 3:8). He walked along the paths with them, talked to them, and taught His perspective on the brand new world they had entered. They had it all yet they needed time with God. We live in a less-than-perfect environment. How much more do we need Him?

A regular quiet time filled with Bible reading, prayer, worship, and meditation is vital to your Christian life.

Relationship and fellowship with God are powered by daily doses of time with Him. Spending time with God brightens my day, comforts, motivates, nourishes, and changes me.

It is more than a quiet time; it is a time of renewal and victory. It is a devil-defeating, heart-comforting, soul-awakening, action-producing, God-revealing, day-brightening, spirit-nourishing, mind-motivating, and life-changing quiet time.

Devil-defeating

Satan is alive and well. His mission is destruction. We can be victorious over him by God's power, power obtained by regularly spending time with God. Lao Tzu, sixth century philosopher, said, "For the mind that is still, the whole universe surrenders." He was right. When we take time to sit still with God and listen to Him, the enemy is defeated.

Heart-comforting

We suffer from illness, pain, loneliness, and stress. Yet God comforts us during our daily quiet time. Only He can relieve our weary hearts

Soul-awakening

Our souls need exercise and energizing. Spending time with Him exposes His viewpoint for us to see and embrace.

Action-producing

God gives each believer a ministry. He reveals it during daily time with Him. He intends for us to be active and moving in the direction He is leading. It's strange, when I spend time with God, I am satisfied, but when I don't, I'm quickly miserable. When I spend time with God, He stretches the hours in the day so that I can fit my busy schedule in. Without time with Him, I never get things done, but with time with Him, I finish my to-do list

God-revealing

There are no limits to our awesome God. We observe His majesty, glory, and power during our quiet time. *And I...in righteousness, I will see your face; when I awake I will be satisfied with seeing your likeness* (Psalm 17:15 NIV).

Day-brightening

Days are tough. Jobs are hard. Children are demanding. Like gray winter skies, the days can close in on us, but spending time with Jesus is like bright sunshine peeking through gray clouds.

Spirit-nourishing

Our bodies need food to function. Our spirits need the Word to live. Our spirits need nourishment to flourish. He feeds us when we spend time with Him.

Mind-motivating

Our minds vegetate as the news media tries to think for us and as TV laugh tracks tell us what's funny. Only God stimulates and motivates our creative juices.

Life-changing

No longer dull, routine, or boring, life will be exciting, unexpected, and fascinating if we spend time with Him.

Even if we don't change our activities, He will change our attitudes and our viewpoints if we spend time with Him every day. God begins to permeate every aspect of our lives and we will change. In times of trouble, we will run for the throne instead of the phone. He will be the guide for our future and the One we follow through the jungle of emotions and crises each day.

Do you want excitement in your life? Nothing is as important as your relationship with God, and the way to know Him is through spending time with Him.

CONSCIENCE

Don't mistake conscience for right or wrong. Postmodern worldview sees truth only as we think something is true. An absolute is only absolute if it feels like an absolute.

We'd love to believe this theory. Having no godly standard for comparison appeals to us.

But conscience is a poor guide. Conscience can be swayed easily. Conscience can be seared over. It can become so hard that nothing can penetrate its inflexible exterior. Conscience, all on its own, is not trustworthy.

Conscience is a reliable guide only when the Holy Spirit enlightens it.

> "And the Holy Spirit helps us in our weakness. For example, we don't know what God wants us to pray for. But the Holy Spirit prays for us with groanings that cannot be expressed in words. And the Father who knows all hearts knows what the Spirit is saying, for the Spirit pleads for us believers in harmony with God's own will" (Romans 8:26–27 NLT).

Keeping your conscience sensitive to God is a four-ingredient recipe.

The first ingredient is daily Bible reading. The Word of God reveals God's character and truth. In other words, we can read and relate to the words in the Bible.

The second ingredient is time alone with the Lord. Time is critical to the process of knowing Him. I know you are thinking that you never have enough time and that time passes too quickly. Lives are busy and schedules are tight. But ask yourself if knowing God is a priority with you. If we don't spend time with God, we will fail in our quest for intimacy with Him. When we don't honor God with our time, we are saying that other factors are more important than God.

Rick Husband, commander of the space shuttle Columbia, knew the importance of time with God. He sent an email from space describing his view from the windows of the spacecraft. He saw Earth and the incredible galaxies beyond. He wept and worshiped God. During a space mission, an astronaut's time and actions are prearranged. Almost every move is prescribed by the flight plan. Yet Rick Husband carved out a time for prayer and worship. We can all find time—if time with God is a priority.

After combining Bible reading and time with God, add the third ingredient: listening. Listen to God speak. He may speak through the Bible, a pastor, a writer, or a teacher. But if you don't listen, how will you know His voice? If you have trouble listening, ask God for sensitivity of heart, and God will wake you up to His beauty and power.

Finally, avoid ungodly thoughts. Your mind isn't a garbage bag. It isn't made to hold junk from books, magazines, TV, and radio. If our minds are filled with junk, we can't hold the truths of God too. One has to make room for the other. Just like wet garbage stinks so trash in your mind fouls your heart.

HE TEACHES US FOR A FUTURE PURPOSE

Spending personal time with the Lord prepares us for the future. We may not recognize the importance of all the lessons He is teaching us now and we may not understand why we need to know them, but someday in the future we will need them.

David was the youngest son of Jesse. He had spent all his young life in the hills shepherding the sheep. One morning his father asked him to take food to his brothers on the battlefront.

"Now Jesse said to his son David, "Take this ephah of roasted grain and these ten loaves of bread for your brothers and hurry to their camp. Take along these ten cheeses to the commander of their unit. See how your brothers are and bring back some assurance from them" (1 Samuel 17:17-18, NIV).

David arrived at the camp. He saw and heard the giant Goliath as well as the fear of the soldiers. When David had awakened that morning, he didn't know it was the day he would have to face a giant. With the strength of the Lord, he defeated Israel's enemy.

In verses 33-37, David revealed his secret weapon.

"Saul replied, 'You are not able to go out against this Philistine and fight him; you are only a boy, and he has been a fighting man from his youth.' But David said to Saul, 'Your servant has been keeping his father's sheep. When a lion or a bear came and carried off a sheep from the flock, I went after it, struck it and rescued the sheep from its mouth. When it turned on me, I seized it by its hair, struck it and killed it. Your servant has killed both the lion and the bear; this uncircumcised Philistine will be like one of them, because he has defied the armies of the living God.

The Lord who delivered me from the paw of the lion and the paw of the bear will deliver me from the hand of this Philistine.' Saul said to David, 'Go, and the Lord be with you'" (1 Samuel 17:33-37, NIV).

Yes, David fought a battle that day with the giant, but the real battle had already been won back on the hillside with the sheep when David spent time alone with God. During those alone hours, he learned that he could trust God even though bears and lions might threaten. Since he had experienced the power of God, facing a giant was no more than another opportunity for God to show up.

When you and I wake each morning, we don't know what we will have to face that day. Today might be a day that an accident or a catastrophe will be waiting for us. But we can be victorious if we have been preparing day after day in our daily quiet time. Just as David had gotten to know God, we too can know Him and trust Him.

You and I don't know what is going to happen today, but we know the God who knows. Time in His Word in the morning will equip you for the unexpected, unthinkable, unbelievable, inconceivable, absurd, ridiculous thing that may be waiting around the next corner. If you are prepared with His Word in your heart, you can deal with it.

It doesn't mean you won't hurt and grieve. It doesn't eliminate pain or loss. But the Word of God gives you the unshakable faith you need to live through whatever happens.

DAILY INTAKE

The best way to obtain power and victory is daily intake of His Word. Joshua gives us a recipe for success,

> "Do not let this Book of the Law depart from your mouth; meditate on it day and night, so that you may be careful to do everything written in it. Then you will be prosperous and successful" (Joshua 1:8, NIV).

Just as we must eat food regularly and let it digest, we must also take in spiritual nutrition and apply it to our lives. There is to be no bulimia in the intake of God's Word. We must not gorge on it on Sunday and fail to eat during the week.

Several years ago, I was reading in the Psalms and I stopped at chapter seventeen.

> "O Lord, by your hand save me from such men, from men of this world whose reward is in this life. You still the hunger of those you cherish; their sons have plenty, and they store up wealth for their children. And I—in righteousness I will see your face; when I awake, I will be satisfied with seeing your likeness (Psalm 17:14-15 NIV).

As I was reading these verses, I was especially drawn to two phrases. The first one was the line in verse 14, "You still the hunger of those you cherish." The second phrase that caught my eye was the end of verse 15. "I will be satisfied with seeing your likeness."

As I read those two phrases over and over again, I began to wonder, "What am I hungry for?" What hungers will God make still in me? With what will I be satisfied? I thought it would be a good idea to identify my hunger so I wrote these words in the margin of my Bible:

My Hungers:
- Deep instruction from the Bible
- To know God intimately
- To trust Him
- To share Him through speaking and writing

I hunger to know God. I crave to know Him more fully and completely. I want to discipline myself to a consistent quiet time each day. I've tried and tried and, to be honest, I've also failed and failed. I start but can't keep up the pace. I've tried devotional books. I've tried workbooks. I've tried plans to read the Bible through. Nothing seems to work for me.

I realize I probably can't discipline myself to success day after day, week after week, month after month, year after year by having a daily, quality quiet time with the Lord. But my strength or my discipline that is not required; hunger is required. How hungry am I? What am I willing to do to satisfy that hunger? Will my appetite for the truths of God overcome the interruptions and distractions of living? When will I make time for God?

No self-discipline, organizational technique, or schedule will cause me to know God. Only deep desire wakes me up early to meet Him. Only a longing heart produces consistency. Only passion for Him leads to time with Him.

After a number of years of practicing the techniques and ideas that you will find in this book, I have begun, only just begun, to be satisfied in my quest to know God. My deepest desire of life is to know Him intimately. I want to know Him so well that I will automatically trust Him no matter what situation arises.

If your hunger is deep, if your cravings are real, if your desire is genuine, if your longing is extreme, if your appetite is great … then you will wake up early or you will stay up late. You will want, need, desire, and crave to be alone with God. You will be filled with excited anticipation about the opportunity to visit with the Lord. Then you will not be looking at the clock wondering if you have made it ten minutes; you will be looking at the clock and wondering, *How did that thirty minutes or one hour pass so fast?*

Stop trying to schedule a quiet time. Stop trying to discipline yourself. Stop trying to whip yourself into shape. Instead, work on your desire. Do you really want to know God intimately? Do you really want to spend time with Him? When your desire is right, the discipline follows.

Nothing can satisfy me like Jesus. Nothing compares to knowing Him. No other thing I put into my life is as important as His Word.

In Psalm 15:1, David asked two questions.
> "Lord, who may dwell in your sanctuary?
> Who may live on your holy hill?"

David's desire to know God was greater than his desire to be a great king, a conquering warrior, or a celebrated musician. He wanted to live on God's holy hill.

When our desire to know God is greater than our desire to sleep, watch TV, or keep our schedules full, we too will begin to climb God's holy hill. On top of God's holy hill there is peace. On top of God's holy hill there is security. On top of God's holy hill there is beauty. On top of God's holy hill there is life. On top of God's holy hill there is vision. My desire is to live on God's holy hill. Will you join me there?

Fifty Reasons Why I Desire to Have an Intimate Relationship With God

1) Because without Him there is no hope Psalm 25:21
2) Because He hears my cry for mercy Psalm 6:9
3) Because He is my refuge Psalm 5:11; Psalm 36
4) Because only God gives relief Psalm 4:7
5) Because He shows me my path Psalm 16:11
6) Because when I need Him, He takes charge Psalm 10:14
7) Because He has never forsaken those who seek Him Psalm 9:10
8) Because the words of the Lord are flawless Psalm 12:6
9) Because I can trust in His unfailing love Psalm 13:5
10) Because He has been good to me Psalm 13:6
11) Because apart from Him, I have no good thing Psalm 16:2
12) Because there is joy in His presence Psalm 16:11; Psalm 19:8
13) Because He turns darkness to light Psalm 18:28
14) Because He broadens my path Psalm 18:36
15) Because He gives me strength Psalm 18:32
16) Because His Word is perfect and it revives my soul Psalm 19:7
17) Because it pleases Him Psalm 19:14
18) Because trouble is near Psalm 22:11
19) Because I need to learn to wait on the Lord Psalm 27:14
20) Because I am to ascribe the glory due His name Psalm 29:2
21) Because His anger lasts only a moment but His favor lasts a lifetime Psalm 30:5
22) Because He already knows my trouble Psalm 31:7,9, Psalm 34:19
23) Because my time is in His hands Psalm 31:15
24) Because when I confess, He forgives Psalm 43:5
25) Because He is my hiding place Psalm 32:7
26) Because He is good Psalm 34:8
27) Because He will be close to me when I am brokenhearted Psalm 34:18
28) Because He will fight my battles Psalm 35:1

29) Because He is the fountain of life Psalm 36:9

30) Because I am troubled by my sin Psalm 38:18

31) Because many are the wonders He has planned for me
Psalm 40:5

32) Because having His words in my heart will give me the desire to
do His will Psalm 40:8

33) Because when I am on my knees, I remember His blessings
Psalm 42:4

34) Because He sends light and truth to guide Psalm 43:3

35) Because He brings victory Psalm 44:3

36) Because when I am still, I can know that He is God
Psalm 46:10

37) Because He will be my guide even to the end Psalm 49:14

38) Because I can meditate on His unfailing love Psalm 49:9

39) Because in the day of trouble, He will deliver me
Psalm 49:14-15

40) Because He teaches me wisdom Psalm 51:5

41) Because God is looking down to see if I am looking up to see
Him Psalm 53:2

42) Because He hears my cries Psalm 55:16-17, 22

43) Because I trust in Him Psalm 56:3; Psalm 55:23c

44) Because I can take refuge in the shadow of His wings until the
disaster has passed Psalm 57:1

45) Because God can fulfill His purpose in me Psalm 57:2

46) Because His love is great Psalm 47:10a

47) Because His faithfulness reaches to the skies Psalm 57:10b

48) Because my soul finds rest in God alone Psalm 62:1

49) Because my salvation and my honor depend on Him
Psalm 62:7

50) Because my soul thirsts for Him Psalm 63:1 [2]

WHEN AND WHERE DO I SPEND TIME WITH GOD?

CHAPTER 2

You know when I sit and when I rise; you perceive my thoughts from afar. You discern my going out and my lying down; you are familiar with all my ways.

Psalm 139:2-3

I love a phrase in Psalm 3 where the psalmist speaks about tiny sparrows building a nest. They build *a place near your altar.*

You can prepare a place in your home where you feel near God's altar. God is everywhere. He has no space limitations. He is omnipresent. But we are limited. To have a spot where we consistently meet with God is both comforting and reassuring.

It becomes your place near His altar. When you have experienced His presence over and over in one specific place, you develop confidence He will always be there to meet you. We begin to think of it as our place near His altar.

A friend of mine was pregnant. During her regular checkup, the doctor told her the sad news that her baby's heart was no longer beating. She was shocked and heartbroken and her grief was enormous.

"We need to admit you to the hospital immediately," the doctor said.

"Fine," she said, "but first I must go home."

"Why?" asked the doctor

"To pray," she answered.

She needed time with the Lord, and in her profound grief, she needed to go to her special place near His altar. The place where she met God every morning. The place where she had heard from Him that morning. The place where she knew she could find Him even though she was broken and shattered.

YOUR SPECIAL PLACE

Your place near God's altar should be the most comfortable and beautiful place in your home. Choose a spot that is usually uncluttered so you don't have to straighten it up before you can relax. It may be an easy chair, a sofa, or a sunny spot by a window. It may be in the dining room, which is usually one place that is clean and neat because it isn't used often.

I have a favorite chair. It is comfortable. I feel good sitting there because lots of family pictures and mementos are nearby. The fireplace stands ready for cold mornings and the view of the woods behind my home is spectacular. This place is rarely in disarray. I have good lighting and plenty of space.

I bring juice in my most beautiful goblet and coffee in my favorite cup. My special time and place is as comfortable and elegant as possible.

WHEN SHOULD I SPEND TIME WITH GOD?

An early morning quiet time before you start the hassles of the day prepares you to face the day. I love the stillness and quiet that permeates the house while everyone else is still asleep. I feel rested after a good night's sleep. I am alert and peaceful. Early in the morning with God is spectacular.

Exodus 16 describes how God provided bread, called manna, for the children of Israel each day. They gathered it in the morning. Later in the day, it was gone.

"Each morning everyone gathered as much as he needed, and when the sun grew hot, it melted away" (Exodus 16:21 NIV).

They were required to gather it each day because it spoiled if they tried to save some for the next day.

Gathering knowledge and comfort from God is like gathering manna. We need to gather it every day, early in the day.

Simple, isn't it?

Some of you just felt a twinge of pain and guilt as you read these words. You are not a morning person. You function better at night. You love your sleep—especially early in the morning. My husband is one of you. He believes that if we were supposed to see the sunrise, God would have scheduled it later in the day.

Don't despair. There is good news for you. The Bible illustrates a time for you late-starters, too. Adam and Eve lived in the Garden of Eden in the perfect world God created. God came every day for conversation. He came *in the cool of the evening* (Genesis 3:8, NIV). Their time of communication and fellowship with the Lord was in the evening. And so, dear night person, God will meet with you in the cool of the evening, too.

Pick the time of day for your quiet time according to your body clock. Whichever you are, a morning, evening, or afternoon person, choose the time of day that best fits you.

27

How do you choose?

1) When are you most alert?
2) When are you most likely not to fall asleep?
3) When is the best time for you to be alone?
4) What time of day is consistently available to you?

If you are the mother of small children, you may choose to spend time with God when they are napping. Some mothers trade an hour of babysitting with a friend and use their hour alone for time with God.

If you exercise in the morning, use your cool-down time to spend with the Lord. Usually after exercising, you are uncommonly alert, and it's easy to sit still awhile.

Examine your schedule. Is there a 30-minute TV program that you watch every day? Will you give it up to spend that time with God?

In her book "Disciplines of a Beautiful Woman," Ann Ortlund suggests getting up in the morning, getting completely dressed and then having your quiet time. She wonders if God gets tired of old house robes, hair in curlers, and unbrushed teeth. She may be right, but I like to wake up and immediately go to my quiet time place and stay there until time to get dressed for work. I know that it will take me approximately one hour to get dressed, so I set a deadline in my mind and that's when my quiet time has to end. The earlier I rise, the longer I get to spend with God.

When I start my quiet time is largely up to God. I have asked him to wake me up. I naturally wake up early, but sometimes I wake up even earlier than normal. Every time that happens, I wonder, *Did God wake me up?* If I get up immediately and go to my quiet time place, I always find out He has something special to reveal to me that day. I make it a habit to ask God at bedtime to wake me up in the morning.

Whenever you decide is best for you, that's when you should schedule your quiet time. Early, midday, late. Choose your best time. Make an appointment with God. Don't let your body clock be an excuse. Don't let your busy schedule be an excuse. Don't let anything get in your way. You can find 15 or 30 minutes to be with the Lord. Be still. Make time.

Ask God to slow you down. Ask God to make your hunger for Him greater than the demands of your busy schedule.

Set the same time every day. A routine scheduled appointment will help you be consistent.

Some people have said to me, "I pray in the car on my way to work every day. That's my special time with the Lord!" I think it is wonderful if you pray in your car (as long as you keep your eyes open). I think it is marvelous to pray while you are doing dishes or vacuuming. I treasure those times, too. But if you and I are going to have a devil-defeating, life-changing, quiet time, we must stop everything else and spend uninterrupted, focused time with Him. Choose your time well. It will change your life. Remember it is desire not discipline that will keep you motivated to meet with God every day.

MATERIALS

Quiet time basket or box. Gather all the materials you need in one basket or box and keep it near your quiet time place. Don't use the basket for anything else. Ask your family not to make it a catch-all for magazines or mail. (Yes, it is okay for Mom to have a basket all her own.)

- Zipper bag filled with:
  - Pens
  - Sharpened pencils
  - Colored markers or pencils
- Index cards (assorted colors and sizes)
- Sticky notes in various sizes

- ◆ Reading glasses
- ◆ Small pack of Kleenex
- ◆ Nail file (so you can take care of pesky hangnails without interrupting your quiet time)
- ◆ Bibles (several versions and at least one volume you don't mind marking in)
- ◆ Notebooks (several sizes and types)
- ◆ Pads of paper
- ◆ Your personal topical Bible (See chapter 5)
- ◆ Your personal commentary (See chapter 5)
- ◆ Assorted reference books

READING

CHAPTER 3

Your word, O Lord is eternal; it stands firm in the heavens.
Psalm 119:89

How sweet are your words to my taste, sweeter than honey to my mouth.
Psalm 119:103

It was January 1 and I held a chart in my hand. The chart, cleverly divided into 365 sections, provided a plan to read the Bible. According to the plan, if I read one Old Testament section, one New Testament passage, a Psalm, and a Proverb every day, I would accomplished my goal of reading through the Bible in one year.

My confidence and enthusiasm soared. This year I would do it.

On January 15, I missed a day because of a business trip. On the 16th, time escaped and I only read the New Testament portion. On the 17th, I contracted a virus that lasted a week. By the time the calendar reached February 1, I was hopelessly behind. I'd failed again.

Through the years, I've repeated this scenario over and over never really reading through the whole Bible.

One year I received a gift Bible divided into daily sections. I decided to ignore the dates on the pages and just read one section at a time. Because of my hectic schedule, I didn't read it every day and I didn't finish in one year, but I finally read the Bible all the way through.

Unfortunately, while I accomplished my goal of reading the whole Bible, I failed at understanding, absorbing, or applying the words.

For me, it is far better to read a small portion and fully understand it than to read a larger prescribed section and never remember what I read. For me, it is more important to find teachings that apply to my life than it is to say, "I've read the whole book in one year."

For some personality types, reading a scheduled plan works well. For others, like me, it only causes guilt and failure. I encourage you to discover what kind of reading plan works for you.

GOD—MY PERSONAL TRAINER

When Paul wrote his second letter to young Timothy. He said,

> "All Scripture is God-breathed and is useful for teaching, rebuking, correcting, and training in righteousness, so that the man of God may be thoroughly equipped for every good work" (2 Timothy 3:16, NIV).

If I read the words of the Bible considering the truth and the instruction it contains, God acts as my personal trainer every day. Just as the goal of a personal trainer is to build his client's body to be strong and healthy, God's goal as our personal trainer is that we may be thoroughly equipped for every good work. The personal trainer uses nutrition, exercise, and weights to do his work. God our personal trainer uses His words, which are alive and powerful, to build us into people who are ready and able to do every good work.

God gave us the Scriptures. In fact, Scripture is the breath of God exhaled out to us so that we can breathe it in. God encourages us to inhale deeply as we train with Him. When we inhale Scripture into our hearts, it generates purpose and vision.

Teaching

Scripture teaches what we do not know. In fact, Scripture gives us knowledge of things we cannot know on our own. God tells us what He wants us to know and how to act in ways that are pleasing to Him. Scripture teaches us how to encourage others and how to lead others to Him.

Rebuking

Scripture exposes the bad attitudes we bottle up inside and the wrong paths we pursue. As we read the living, breathing words of God, our lives are changed from the inside out. Our viewpoint changes. Our disposition is revised. Our temperament is altered. Our approach is corrected.

Correcting

Fortunately Scripture doesn't stop with rebuke; it not only corrects our wrong behaviors, it offers alternatives. Scripture shows us that we don't have to live apart from God. We can come into His presence and know Him. We can understand what displeases Him and what pleases Him. And we can change.

Training

As a personal trainer teaches his client to stay away from poor food choices and enjoy good nutritious foods, so God, as our personal trainer, guides our steps away from the harmful and takes us to the highest level of spiritual fitness.

READING IS REWARDING

Action-oriented Americans like to work and accomplish goals. Even our leisure activities have become work. We strive to exercise properly, have the perfect yard, or be the best at our favorite sport. We fail to read because reading seems like wasting time, as if we haven't made any progress or accomplished any goal.

In addition, active lifestyles eliminate time to read. We have so much to do or so many places to go that we don't think we can sit still long enough to read.

The time-crunch affects every age group. College students fill their lives with classes, sports, social events, and studying with no time to spare. Couples with young children meet themselves coming and going to soccer games, football and baseball practices, music lessons, school and church activities. Swamped with jobs, home care, travel, and grandchildren, middle-aged couples struggle for time. Singles and single parents never have enough time to do all they want and need to do much less time for themselves. Retired folks are busy with social activities, traveling, and extended family. All age groups find it difficult to carve out time to read.

Join these complicated lives with the fact that many people don't read well, the result is a culture of non-readers.

Difficulties range from needing glasses to dyslexia. Others have been poorly trained. Some teaching methods of the last three decades have not fostered good reading skills.

In addition, media stimulation such as radio, television, and computers make reading unnecessary. When you factor in poor comprehension, it is no surprise our nation does not like to read.

How can we solve the problem of disinterest, dislike, and personal difficulty when we tackle reading our Bible?

BIBLE TRANSLATIONS

The first step is to get a Bible that helps instead of hinders your reading. A Bible written on your reading level is essential if you are going to enjoy or understand what you read. Choose a simple, modern language version or paraphrase, or choose traditional poetic old English translations. What really matters is that you actually read it and that in the reading, you grasp the meaning.

Some of the more recent popular translations will help you. They approach scripture in various ways. Without arguing the merits of the translation,[4] let's look at the language differences. This information may help you choose a translation that will work for you. [5]

King James Version (KJV)

The King James Version is lyrical and conservative. Some language in the KJV is archaic and hard to understand. Other parts of the KJV are poetic and flowing. It contains the most familiar wording to thousands of people and is loved by generations. The KJV is easy to memorize because of the rhythmical flow of the words. It is written on a twelfth-grade reading level.

New King James Version (NKJV)

This fine translation retains the poetic and familiar language of the KJV, but many of the hardest words are updated to more common and understandable verbiage. However, it is still difficult in some passages. The NKJV is written on a ninth-grade reading level.

New International Version (NIV)

The NIV is one of the most popular modern translations. Millions of copies have been sold worldwide. It is easy to read. The translators used careful sentence structure to carry the thoughts to the mind of the reader. The NIV is a translation of thoughts and phrases so the result is an easy flow of the paragraphs. It is written on the reading level of mid-year seventh grade.

New Century Version (NCV)

The easy-to-read New Century Version uses contemporary English. The translation converts the truths of the Bible into language that can be understood by readers. Some passages in the NCV lose the poetic beauty that is so loved in other translations because of its common language. However, as you read the NCV you will begin to understand some passages that you haven't really seen clearly before – a result of the simple language style. The vocabulary is approximately third-grade level and the version avoids long sentences.

New American Standard Bible (NASB)

The NASB is perhaps one of the most literal translations. Using a word-for-word technique, the translators converted words from the original language to English. This task was complicated because English does not have as many descriptive words nor the same sentence structure. Word-for-word translation isn't practical and some nuances of the original language may be lost in the process simply because an English word can't fully describe the meaning. For example, in Greek there are numerous words for love, including eros, philao, and agape, all of which describe a different aspect for the one English word "love."

Since the NASB has attempted to translate word for word in a literal fashion, the English result is a choppy sentence structure. Even though you will likely be pleased with the translation's accuracy, you may stumble over the harder to read paragraphs. The reading level is approximately eleventh grade.

The Message (THE MESSAGE)

Filled with refreshing phrase and unusual language twists, Eugene Petersen's new contemporary English paraphrase is a delight to read. Every reading will stimulate your thoughts. As I read this translation, I am often impressed by the fresh words. I usually smile because Petersen has given me a new outlook on a familiar passage or because he has caused me to think of God in a way I've never considered before. The reading level is fourth to fifth grade.

The Living Bible (LB)

Kenneth Taylor paraphrased the epistles so his ten children could understand the Bible. Originally published as the Living Letters, Taylor eventually paraphrased the entire Bible. The result is a good readable Bible. I like to read the Living Bible before going to bed. It is easy to read and the fresh use of words is helpful in understanding the whole of each passage. It is written in eighth-grade reading level language.

The New Living Translation (NLT)

This is an actual translation not a paraphrase as in the Living Bible. Written on a sixth-grade reading level, the editors used modern, up-to-date language to produce an invigorating and enjoyable edition.

The Amplified Bible (AMP)

The Amplified Bible adds descriptive words throughout each chapter. The added words provide helpful definitions and enhancements. Even with some cumbersome sentence structures of the older English, the definitions provide invaluable help with difficult passages. All added words are placed within parentheses throughout the translation.

As you compare the following verse in the various translations mentioned above, you clearly see the differences in the language usage. However, you can also see that the meaning of the verse is the same in each one. In the verse, John makes the statement that Jesus is the Word of God and that He came to earth to live in the flesh. None of the translations leaves those facts in doubt. As you read this verse several times, consider the flow of the words, the beauty of the words, how the words express the truth, then pick your preferred style.

John 1:14

KJV: "And the Word was made flesh, and dwelt among us, (and we beheld his glory, the glory as of the only begotten of the Father,) full of grace and truth."

NKJV: "And the Word became flesh and dwelt among us, and we beheld His glory, the glory as of the only begotten of the Father, full of grace and truth."

NIV: "The Word became flesh and made his dwelling among us. We have seen his glory, the glory of the one and only Son, who came from the Father, full of grace and truth."

NCV: "The Word became a human and lived among us. We saw his glory—the glory that belongs to the only Son of the Father—and he was full of grace and truth."

NASB: "And the Word became flesh, and dwelt among us, and we beheld His glory, glory as of the only begotten from the Father, full of grace and truth."

THE MESSAGE: "The Word became flesh and blood, and moved into the neighborhood. We saw the glory with our own eyes, the one-of-a-kind glory, like Father, like Son, generous inside and out, true from start to finish."

LB: "And Christ became a human being and lived here on earth among us and was full of loving forgiveness and truth. Some of us have seen his glory – the glory of the only Son of the heavenly Father!"

NLT: "So the Word became human and made his home among us. He was full of unfailing love and faithfulness. And we have seen his glory, the glory of the Father's one and only Son."

AMP: "And the Word (Christ) became flesh (human, incarnate) and tabernacled (fixed his tent of flesh, lived awhile) among us; and we [actually] saw His glory (His honor, His majesty), such glory as an only begotten son receives from his father, full of grace (favor, loving-kindness) and truth."

The different words used by the modern translators do not change the meaning of the verse, but they do make the verse clearer or more thought provoking. In some translations, Christ is called the Word. In others, he is called Christ. We are told he dwelt with us, lived among us, lived here on earth, tabernacled among us, or moved into our neighborhood. These different phrases help us comprehend that he came to earth to live as a human being. Now people with all levels of reading skills and preferences can read, understand, and enjoy the Bible.

Make it a priority in your life to find a readable translation for your quiet time. Consider your personal language skills, vocabulary, personality, and preferences. Are you quick? Slow? Patient? Impatient? Willing to spend extra time finding definitions or want them already defined for you? Combine all these factors to determine which Bible rendition is perfect for you. Eventually, like me, you may want to build your library to contain a copy of each one.

PARAGRAPHS

Reading in paragraph-sized chunks will increase your comprehension. Paragraphs allow you to stop at the end of each thought and review what you've read. Did you see what the author was saying? Did you understand the context? Did you read something that seems to apply to your life today?

If your Bible translation doesn't have paragraphs, block off a small number of verses to read. Digest each segment before moving on to the next. Ask yourself if the author is building to a conclusion. Does one sentence enhance the sentence before it? Does that sentence lead you to the next conclusion?

CLUE WORDS

Look for clue words throughout the scripture. Clue words help you discover the author's point. For example, if you see the word "therefore," the author is about to tell you his conclusion based on the facts presented in the previous verses. So it is a good idea to look back at the last few verses and review what has been said. Or as we often say to our Explore-the-Bible group, "When you see the word 'therefore,' be sure you figure out what it's there for."

Notice how focus on the clue word helps in the following verse: *There will always be poor people in the land.* ***Therefore,*** *I command you to be openhanded toward your brothers and toward the poor and needy in your land* (Deuteronomy 15:11 NIV).

"Therefore" is the clue word. God commands us to be openhanded. Why? Because there will always be poor people in the land. "Therefore" is the pivot point. It is true that poor people are with us and God expects us to do something about it.

"Nevertheless" is another clue word. When you see the word, expect to see a contrast. You should look at the sentences before and after the clue word to get a full understanding.

In 2 Chronicles, you can see how this technique is helpful. ***Nevertheless,*** *you are not the one to build the temple, but your son, who is your own flesh and blood — he is the one who will build the temple for my name* (2 Chronicles 6:9, NIV).

God told David it was a good idea to build a temple but David wouldn't be allowed to do it. God would, however (nevertheless) allow David's son to do the construction.

"But" is also used as a clue word. When you see it, know the author is going to give you more facts or suggest another action. Pay attention to the words that follow. You will usually learn a principle. Look at this verse from Psalms: *The wicked borrow and do not repay,* **but** *the righteous give generously* (Psalm 37:21 NIV).

See the contrasts between the wicked and the righteous separated by the clue word "but"? The psalmist said, *I do not trust in my bow, my sword does not bring me victory;* **but** *you give us victory over our enemies, you put our adversaries to shame* (Psalm 44:6-7 NIV). See how God brings victory not self-effort. The clue word shows the contrast.

One of my favorite Bible clues is the phrase "but God." I mark that two-word phrase wherever I see it in the Bible because I know that I'm about to read how God intervened into man's life situation. The exciting thing about learning what God has done in certain situations is that I usually can see more clearly how God will work in my life, too.

Read the following examples of the "but God" clue.

"You intended to harm me, **but God** intended it for good to accomplish what is now being done, the saving of many lives" (Genesis 50:20 NIV).

"Very rarely will anyone die for a righteous man, though for a good man someone might possibly dare to die. **But God** demonstrates his own love for us in this: While were still sinners, Christ died for us" (Romans 5:7-8 NIV).

In these examples, the clue words **"but God"** demonstrate how God intervened in impossible situations. Joseph's awful situation turned good when God intervened. In the Romans passage, Paul describes how God loved us when were unlovable and died for us when we deserved death. "But God." How wonderful that God intervenes in our lives!

ACTION WORDS

Remember diagramming sentences when you were in junior high language arts class? One of the things you looked for was the verb —the action word. As you read the Bible, make it a habit to find the action words. These words often explain what God wants you to do.

"Submit yourselves, then, to God. Resist the devil, and he will flee from you. Come near to God and he will come near to you. Wash your hands, you sinners, and purify your hearts, you double-minded. Grieve, mourn and wail. Change your laughter to mourning and your joy to gloom. Humble yourselves before the Lord and he will lift you up" (James 4:7-10 NIV).

There are ten action words in these few verses.
- Submit
- Resist
- Come near
- Wash
- Purify
- Grieve
- Mourn
- Wail
- Change
- Humble yourself

As you notice these action words, ask yourself these questions: What is God asking from me? To what does He want me to submit? What do I need to resist? He is calling me to come near; have I? Am I washed? Am I purified? About what is He asking me to grieve, mourn, or wail? My sins? My failures? How does He want me to change? Am I willing to completely humble myself before Him in order to follow Him?

Identifying the action words can help you not only understand a scripture but help you to apply it to your life.

READING UNTIL GOD SPEAKS

Begin reading each day's passage by asking God to speak to you. It is a simple yet profound prayer: *Lord, even if I only read three words, make them impact my life today.*

Most days I start reading and stop when God speaks to me through the words on the page. I have learned to read until God stops me on a verse. The most amazing insight happens. I'll be reading along and suddenly a certain word or phrase will penetrate my mind. Then I know I have reached a point of contact with Him. The Holy Spirit will use the phrase to touch my heart and change my life pattern.

When I reach that point, I know He is ready to speak to me. I always stop and sit still for a while so that I can hear what He is saying.

Sometimes I may read several chapters before I come to that point of hearing God speak. Other times it may be only one verse. It really doesn't matter how many verses or chapters I read each day. It isn't the quantity that interests me. What does matter is that I hear from God about my current situation.

For me, hearing from God is not an audible sound but a feeling in my heart and mind that if I will ponder His Word at that particular phrase or section, the Holy Spirit will teach me a new lesson and help me.

MARK YOUR BIBLE

In the next chapter you will learn methods to write as you read so we won't cover them here, but I do want to mention marking your

Bible. I have tried numerous kinds of markers from highlighters and colored pens to pencils and colored pencils.

You may want to experiment with various types of pens, highlighters, and pencils to find what works best for you. Colored pencils work best for me. They mark the passage smoothly and the color does not bleed through the thin Bible paper. With pencils, I have no fear of an ink leak or spill when I travel. They are easily sharpened and don't dry out with use.

As I read I usually hold in my hand six pencils: red, pink, yellow, brown, green, and blue. If I like a phrase or see a list in a verse, or realize a truth, I can mark the words with one of these colors. Then as I go back over the same verses (even on a different day), I focus on the marked phrases.

After a long time of reading and marking, your Bible can become cluttered with marks. These marks will help you find verses that have special meaning or certain passages you want to remember.

I treasure my Bible and its markings. Once when I bought a new Bible, I spent months transferring all the notes and markings from my old Bible to the new one.

I love those markings, but I have also discovered that if I am reading a passage that is well-marked and highlighted, my eyes and my brain tend to go directly to those verses already marked. This is good to help me remember what I've learned before, but sometimes I realize that I am passing over the verses in between just because of a trick of my eyes. When this happens, I solve the problem by reading a different, un-marked Bible. In the Christian bookstore, there are numerous inexpensive Bibles. Some are paperback editions which only cost a few dollars and are perfect for this purpose.

DEVOTIONAL GUIDES

A devotional guide is an excellent way to focus on a subject or passage of scripture. Devotional guides bend your thoughts in God's direction. Most guides have a verse, the writer's comments, a story, an application, and a prayer response. A devotional guide will push your thoughts beyond the ordinary.

More often than not, the daily passage will lead me to look for additional places to read and ponder.

If you are like me, however, a daily devotional guide is sometimes a tool to produce guilt, because I can't seem to read and complete every page every single day. Some days I am so interested in a different passage that I don't pick up the devotional book at all that day. Then I get a feeling of guilt because I have blank pages or a missed date.

So to alleviate guilt, I change the dates. A devotional guide might last several years using this system. I can also read from several different authors during the year if I ignore the dates. Some days I might read two or three devotionals and others I may read none. All I have to do to make this work is change the dates.

Re-dating the pages myself may seem like a simple, trivial matter but doing it seems to satisfy my sense of order without tying me to a particular book every day. And it eases my guilt feelings. Not only that but I can successfully read the writings of numerous authors during the course of a year. Having this freedom allows my creative nature to be free to try various quiet time methods frequently.

READ THE WORD

In his book "The Mind of Christ," T.W. Hunt said that when he embarked on his journey to know Christ completely, he determined that he would not read anything except the Bible for one year.

He didn't read a book, a newspaper, or anything except the Bible. It was a thrilling experiment for him as he began to know God in a more real way. The result is his wonderful study on becoming like Christ.

I am not suggesting that you also take a vow like T.W. Hunt because only God can call you to a commitment like that. But it is important for you and me to understand that we must read the Bible if we are going to know God.

Pamphlets, devotional guides, commentaries, study guides, and such materials are important and we should read good solid Christian writers. Christian materials bring insight and help us become doctrinally sound. Books, magazines, articles, and study guides will strengthen our Christian lives, cause us to stand strong in the face of trials, help us when we feel confused or dismayed. They are good and needed. But don't forget to read the Bible. In other words, if we aren't careful, we can spend a lot of time reading about the Bible and not the Bible itself. It is a matter of balance.

For instance, I could tell you the story of David and Goliath. I would tell you about the young boy who went to see his brothers at the war camp and was shocked to see a giant threatening and challenging the Israelites. I could tell you about how he picked up five little stones and bravely, with the Lord's help, killed the giant. You would love the story. You might be thrilled to see how God protected and saved Israel by the courage of a young boy. It would be good for you to know and you would learn truth and principles. But if you read the story for yourself, you would see all the other characters in the story. Saul, the king who tried to get David to fight in his armor. The brothers who mocked and teased young David. The giant who challenged for forty days and laughed when a child came after him.

Through these details, you would learn additional principles such as: *Be yourself. Wear your own armor. Do what God tells you to do instead of following public opinion. God fulfills His purposes through people, even a small child.*

You can see how important it is for you to read the verses yourself and let God teach you through His words to you.

PSALMS READING PLAN

Years ago, someone told me that since there are 150 Psalms you could read five each day and in a thirty-day month, you would read them all. The thought really intrigued me so one day I made the chart you see on the next page. I started with the day of the month then read that Psalm.

Then I added thirty and read that Psalm. Then I added thirty more and read that Psalm. Then I added thirty more and read that Psalm. Finally I added thirty to the date again and read the last of the five Psalms for the day.

As you look at the chart, you will see that it assists you in reading the Psalms using this plan. In the left column is the day of the month. On each day, you are to read five Psalms. In each thirty-day period, you will read the entire book of Psalms by following this chart.

On the first of the month, you read chapters 1, 31, 61, 91, and 121. On the twenty-sixth day of the month, you read 26, 56, 86, 116, and 146. One thing that really amazes me is how the five Psalms for each day under this plan relate to each other and complement each other.

Date	Chapters......	....	....	....
1	1	31	61	91	121
2	2	32	62	92	122
3	3	33	63	93	123
4	4	34	64	94	124
5	5	35	65	95	125
6	6	36	66	96	126
7	7	37	67	97	127
8	8	38	68	98	128
9	9	39	69	99	129
10	10	40	70	100	130
11	11	41	71	101	131
12	12	42	72	102	132
13	13	43	73	103	133
14	14	44	74	104	134
15	15	45	75	105	135
16	16	46	76	106	136
17	17	47	77	107	137
18	18	48	78	108	138
19	19	49	79	109	139
20	20	50	80	110	140
21	21	51	81	111	141
22	22	52	82	112	142
23	23	53	83	113	143
24	24	54	84	114	144
25	25	55	85	115	145
26	26	56	86	116	146
27	27	57	87	117	147
28	28	58	88	118	148
29	29	59	89	119	149
30	30	60	90	120	150

While I haven't read the five Psalms every single day in all these years, I have read through the book of Psalms hundreds of times using this plan. Because the passage is tied to the date, no matter where I am in the world, I can look at the calendar and know which Psalms I am supposed to read today. I turn to the Psalm for today's date and then add thirty to that number and read the next Psalm until I have read all five for the day.

I like to call this my "no guilt" plan because I can read in Psalms one day and if for some reason I don't read in Psalms again for several days, I can simply re-start immediately on the current date. Since one reading is not affected by the previous reading, I am free to read only today's verses. No guilt.

ADD PROVERBS

According to 1 Kings 4:29-32, King Solomon spoke more than 3,000 proverbs. The Bible records some of these wisdom sayings in the book of Proverbs.

Through these true statements, we gain insight into God's nature and learn how to live with others.

There are 31 chapters in Proverbs, which can be added one day at a time to the Psalms chart. Read one chapter on the day of the month it represents. Read Proverbs 5 on December 5 and Proverbs 25 on January 25, for example.

READ THROUGH A BOOK

One of the most interesting ways to read the Bible is to read a whole book of the Bible in one reading. With the goal of understanding what we read, reading a whole book helps us see the whole picture of the book.

Start with 1 John. It isn't too long and every verse is a treasure. Several years ago, someone challenged me to read 1 John every day for a month. I did and it was such a great experience that I kept reading. I read the book 90 days in a row. The book made an enormous impact on my life and on my understanding of God.

Look at these verses from this amazing book:

> "This is the message we have heard from him and declare to you: God is light; in him there is no darkness at all" (1 John 1:5 NIV).

> "For everything in the world – the cravings of sinful man, the lust of his eyes and the boasting of what he has and does – comes not from the Father but from the world" (1 John 2:16 NIV).

> "How great is the love the Father has lavished on us, that we should be called children of God! And that is what we are! The reason the world does not know us is that it did not know him" (1 John 3:1 NIV).

You might want to start reading a whole book by reading the book of Ruth. It is a great love story and a wonderful example of God's love to us. Put yourself in Ruth's shoes. Try to understand how she felt when her husband died. How frustrated did she get when she had to take care of her mother-in-law? Why did she go back to Israel with her mother-in-law? Would you be embarrassed to pick up grain like a beggar?

Deuteronomy is another book to read all the way through (you may need to divide it into three readings). When I first started to read Deuteronomy, I thought it would be full of hard-to-understand laws and even harder names, but I was surprised! It is a book of encouragement. I have read it about 50 times. It is practically my favorite book. Look at some of the incredible verses found in Deuteronomy.

"Do not be afraid of them; the Lord your God himself will fight for you" (Deuteronomy 3:22 NIV).

"You were shown these things so that you might know that the Lord is God; besides him there is no other" (Deuteronomy 4:35 NIV).

"Oh, that their hearts would be inclined to fear me and keep all my commands always, so that it might go well with them and their children forever" (Deuteronomy 5:29 NIV).

READ ON A SPECIFIC SUBJECT

Using the alphabetical index of a concordance, find a subject that you want to know more about. Make a list of every verse about that subject and then read each one. This is a way to broaden your view of any subject and to be sure that what you think you know about that subject really did or did not come from the Bible. I would like to suggest several subjects:

Angels

Angels are real beings. They have a special ministry to believers and to unbelievers. They are especially interested in women. Why? Who are they? Where do they come from? What do they do?

There is so much interest in angels. In book and gift stores, you will find figurines, plaques, books, poems, and all kinds of things about angels. If you read some of the poems or books, you will get very confused about who they are and what they are doing in our world. But you can find out the whole truth about them if you look up and read all the verses on angels in the Bible. Whatever you read in the Bible about angels is true, and you can depend on those facts.

<u>Faith</u>

Another interesting subject is faith. What is real faith? I am convinced that it is somehow connected with waiting. Why do I think that?

Because I have read about Sarah and Abraham waiting for a child. I have seen how Paul waited to see God work in the churches Paul planted. I have read about Moses waiting forty years in the desert until God was ready to start Moses in his ministry. You can learn these kinds of things if you read every verse about faith in the Bible.

Use your exhaustive concordance to read every verse on the following subjects:

* Clean/Cleanse   * Eye
* Sun   * Peace
* Father   * Heart
* God's right hand * Mountain
* Oath

READ WITH UNDERSTANDING

<u>Look</u>

As we read a passage, our first step is to look at and identify the facts in the passage. Observe carefully. Determine who is speaking. Who is he speaking to? Then notice the style. Is it firm or angry? Perhaps it is instructive. Does it have a surface meaning and a deeper teaching tucked in too?

One exercise that helps me is to jot down the facts in bullet point fashion. For example, I would make the following list of bullet points when I read Ephesians 4:1-6.

"As a prisoner for the Lord, then, I urge you to live a life worthy of the calling you have received. Be completely humble and gentle; be patient, bearing with one another in love. Make every effort to keep the unity of the Spirit through the bond of peace. There is one body and one Spirit – just as you were called to one hope when you were called – one Lord, one faith, one baptism, one God and Father of all, who is over all and through all and in all" (NIV).

- Paul is a prisoner
- Live a worthy life
- Be humble, gentle, and patient
- Love one another
- Keep the unity in peace
  - One body
  - One Spirit
  - One hope
  - One Lord
  - One faith
  - One baptism
  - One God
  - One Father

Once I have made these bullet points, I can begin to understand what the author is trying to say. Then I ask questions. Is there an obvious point? Is there a secondary point? Does the author bring up any questions? If so, does he answer them? I read it again to see if he mentions any controversies. Does he mention any groups of people? What does he say about them? Are there any contrasts? As I notice these things, I begin to read with understanding. Often all it takes is simply looking carefully at the text as I read it.

Try this exercise:

"Lord, who may dwell in your sanctuary? Who may live on your holy hill? He whose walk is blameless and who does what is righteous, who speaks the truth from his heart and has no slander on his tongue, who does his neighbor no wrong and casts no slur on his fellowman, who despises a vile man but honors those who fear the Lord, who keeps his oath even when it hurts, who lends his money without usury and does not accept a bribe against the innocent. He who does these things will never be shaken" (Psalm 15:1-5 NIV).

What is the Psalmist's first question? [6]

What does he ask? [7]

What three action verbs answer the question?[8]

What three things must we not do?[9]

Name three things a man must have.[10]

We are looking at the scripture, observing what it says. At this point, we are not trying to analyze what it says nor are we trying to do what it says, we are simply looking at what it says.

See

We have already looked at the facts in the passage. Now we need to look deeper into the passage and try to understand what lesson is being taught. What does the author mean when he says what he says?

What does the author want us to learn? When he lists steps to do or sins to resist, what is the intent? Does the passage present a principle for us to learn? Can we form a central truth from what we read? In the Psalm example above, as we interpret the meaning of the words, we see that dwelling close to God and living on His mountain require some effort on our parts. To live on God's holy hill means we must remove some activities and mindsets from our lives. We can't continue to slander our neighbors and do wrong to people we meet if we expect to be in perfect communion with the Lord.

In the beginning, the "see" step may not seem easy and you may want to give up. Keep trying and it will become easier and easier. First you will become more familiar with the Bible and second you will become better at finding the lesson.

Commentaries and dictionaries are very helpful here, but before you open one of these helps, try to discover the facts and lessons on your own.

Also, take plenty of time on each passage you read. You don't have to impose a quota of verses to read every day. Begin with just a paragraph or a part of a chapter. Don't move on until you really understand what is being said and why.

Know

The third step is probably the most important. After we have looked at the verses and after we have seen into them, then we begin to know what the words means to us personally. This step helps us apply the truth of the teaching of the passage.

In the Psalm passage, we can clearly know the steps to take to reach the holy mountain of God. Honor and fear the Lord. Live in honesty and fairness with our fellow man.

Example from Colossians:

"We always thank God, the Father of our Lord Jesus Christ, when we pray for you, because we have heard of your faith in Christ Jesus and of the love you have for all the saints – the faith and love that spring from the hope that is stored up for you in heaven and that you have already heard about in the word of truth, the gospel that has come to you. All over the world this gospel is bearing fruit and growing, just as it has been doing among you since the day you heard it and understood God's grace in all its truth. You learned it from Epaphras, our dear fellow servant, who is faithful minister of Christ on our behalf, and who also told us of your love in the Spirit" (Colossians 1:3-8 NIV).

On the surface, when we look at these verses at the beginning of Paul's letter to the Colossians, it appears to be a salutation. He greeted them and told them he was thankful for them. When we read the verses again, we see he was also praying for them. He had heard about their faith and love. He told them they were not alone. All over the world, the gospel produced this kind of love and faith in people and Paul was thrilled.

When we read the paragraph a third time, we begin to know the even deeper level of truth. Paul said that the faith and love in their lives came from the hope they have in Jesus. He reminded them they are people who have been gloriously and miraculously saved.

After reading the passage three times and understanding the layers of truth, we can then apply them to our lives by asking some pointed questions:

- Who do I pray for?
- Do I thank God for people I know?
- Has anyone heard about my faith and love?
- Does anyone know about the hope I have in Jesus?
- If so, how do they know? If not, why not?
- Is it evident in my speech and actions?
- Am I interested in missions?
- Do I do anything to help missions?

You can see that this Look/See/Know plan will take you deeper as you read scriptures.

Example from Hebrews:

"Let us draw near to God with a sincere heart in full assurance of faith, having our hearts sprinkled to cleanse us from a guilty conscience and having our bodies washed with pure water. Let us hold unswervingly to the hope we profess, for he who promised is faithful. And let us consider how we may spur one another on toward love and good deeds. Let us not give up meeting together, as some are in the habit of doing, but let us encourage one another – and all the more as you see the Day approaching" (Hebrews 10:22-25 NIV).

Five times the writer says, "Let us." Mark these five phrases with the numbers 1, 2, 3, 4, and 5. Find two clue words in verses 19 and 21.[11] Ask yourself personal questions using the action words:

Where do I **draw near?**
What do I **hold** on to?
How am I to **consider?**
What should I **not give up** on?
Who should I **encourage?**

57

SOME HELPFUL HINTS TO REMEMBER

- Read small sections at a time to apply this technique.
- A Bible which has paragraphs is helpful.
- Re-read the paragraph at least twice and more often to <u>see</u> the under-the-surface truths.
- Ask questions like:
    - Do I do the things it says to do?
    - Do I measure up to the levels of maturity in this passage?
- Look for clue words.
- Make lists.
- Draw conclusions.

Pray at the beginning of your study and at the end of each passage. Ask God to show you what you need to know.

HOW TO FIND THE APPLICATIONS

According to 2 Timothy 3:16, all scripture is given for one of four reasons: Showing us truth; exposing our rebellion; correcting our mistakes; and training us to live God's way

Look for at least one of these factors in every paragraph that you read. Paul said that all scripture would do these things. Every passage is in the Bible for the purpose of doctrine, reproof, instruction, and/or training. Finding the purpose of a passage will help you understand the meaning.

Using the three examples given above from Psalms, Colossians, and Hebrews you can determine the reason for these passages. Is it doctrine, reproof, instruction, and/or training?

MARGIN REFERENCES

Look at the margins in your Bible. On the sides or down the middle of each page, the publisher has included the location of related verses as a help in understanding words and phrases in the passage. It is worthwhile to look up each one as you read.

DRAWING A VISUAL PICTURE

As you read, try to draw a visual picture of the passage to help you understand the verse. For instance, in Philippians 2:5-11 we are told of the attitude of Christ. He left heaven and came to earth to die on the cross for us. Then we are told how God elevated Him back to His former glory. You can visualize these verses as two staircases. In verses 5-8, you see a down staircase with seven steps of how Jesus lowered Himself to earth.

"Your attitude should be the same as that of Christ Jesus: Who being in very nature God, did not consider equality with God something to be grasped, but made himself nothing, taking the very nature of a servant, being made in human likeness. And being found in appearance as a man, he humbled himself and became obedient to death – even death on a cross!" (NIV).

And then in verses 9-11, you see the upward staircase of God exalting Jesus.

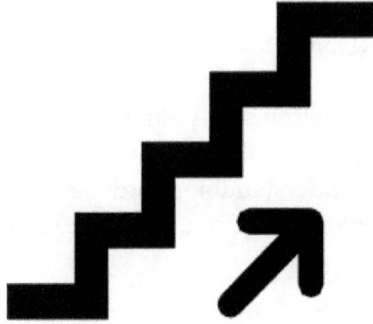

"Therefore God exalted him to the highest place and gave him the name that is above every name, that at the name of Jesus every knee should bow, in heaven and on earth and under the earth, and every tongue confess that Jesus Christ is Lord, to the glory of God the Father" (NIV).

When I first visualized this passage of Scripture as a down and up staircase I realized I would never forget the meaning of the verses. I have used this visual aid in many talks and explanations of what Christ has done. The visual image will often stay with us longer than the words we read. There are passages of Scripture you can visualize as a circle, a box, a tree, a root, a sail, etc. If you put these visual labels on the passages you will retain the meaning in your mind.

DIVINE VIEWPOINT – DVP

When reading scripture, I often ask, *Is there anything here that shows the difference between how God sees and how I see.* Is there a divine viewpoint? If I do see a God-view, I mark it with the letters "DVP" for divine viewpoint. In my humanity, I rarely catch a glimpse of God's perspective because He is God of the universe who can see the end from the beginning. Marking the passage with these three letters reminds me of my limitations and of His wisdom.

REPEATED WORDS

To determine the author's emphasis in the passage, look for repeated words. In 2 Corinthians 3, the words "ministry" and "ministers" are mentioned six times in verses 3-9.

> "You show that you are a letter from Christ, the result of our ministry, written not with ink but with the Spirit of the living God, not on tablets of stone but on tablets of human hearts. Such confidence as this is ours through Christ before God. Not that we are competent in ourselves to claim anything for ourselves, but our competence comes from God. He has made us competent as ministers of a new covenant – not of the letter but of the Spirit, for the letter kills, but the Spirit gives life.
>
> Now if the ministry that brought death, which was engraved in letters on stone, came with glory, so that the Israelites could not look steadily at the face of Moses because of its glory, fading though it was, will not the ministry of the Spirit be even more glorious? If the ministry that condemns men is glorious, how much more glorious is the ministry that brings righteousness" (2 Corinthians 3:3-9 NIV)

Who are the ministers mentioned? What do the ministers do? Where does the ministry have results? What is the benefit of the ministry? Repeated words direct us to the focus of the passage.

In Romans 1:1-17, the word "gospel" is repeated six times. In your journal, describe the gospel according to these verses. What is the meaning of the word? What does the writer say about it? How can the gospel help? How can you spread the gospel?

DEFINITIONS

The Bible will often give you a beautiful definition of important words. The definitions may be a sentence as in Hebrews 11:1 where the writer defines faith: *Now faith is being sure of what we hope for and certain of what we do not see.*

The definition may be a surprising word picture as in 1 John 5:4 where we are told that faith is the victory. *For everyone born of God overcomes the world. This is the victory that has overcome the world, even our faith.*

Looking for these kinds of word pictures helps you understand the scriptures. In the next chapter on writing, there are ideas about how to record definitions and other insights for future reference.

SECLUDED FACTS

Look for facts and insights that are not obvious. Think through events as if they are happening right now in real time. For example, in Acts 3, Peter and John meet a man who had been crippled from birth. During their conversation, the man was healed. As you think this through carefully and look for secluded facts, you realize that there are two miracles in this story. He not only had his legs healed but he began to walk instantly. No physical therapy was required. He jumped up to walk. Finding secluded facts will not only help you understand but will bless you with new insights into the nature, power, and character of God.

PRINCIPLES FOR LIFE—PFL

Adopting "Principles for Life" in scripture is the art of applying a belief, value, or standard from the passage to modern life. Finding life lessons in a passage of Scripture is not easy but it is possible by careful reading. Try finding the life lesson in John 20:3-9 as the events of the morning of the crucifixion are described:

> "So Peter and the other disciple started for the tomb. Both were running, but the other disciple outran Peter and reached the tomb first. He bent over and looked in at the strips of linen lying there but did not go in. Then Simon Peter, who was behind him, arrived and went into the tomb. He saw the strips of linen lying there, as well as the burial cloth that had been

around Jesus' head. The cloth was folded up by itself, separate from the linen. Finally the other disciple, who had reached the tomb first, also went inside. He saw and believed. (They still did not understand from Scripture that Jesus had to rise from the dead.)" (NIV).

Peter and John went to the tomb. There was no body. They saw the grave was empty, and they saw the grave clothes lying there but there was no body. Look at the facts. In verses 6 and 8, they saw.

In verse 8, they believed. But verse 9 declares they did not understand. What can you learn? It seems like only a narrative of what happened, but if you think carefully about it, you realize that they couldn't understand what was happening but they believed anyway. One of the principles for life—PFL—is that "believing is not always understanding completely."

You might miss these few words in the passage unless you are reading carefully and slowly analyzing each verse as you go. It helps to make lists of verbs or thoughts or write the facts to help you see what you might otherwise miss.

WHEN SCRIPTURE EMPHASIZES

Jesus said, *Peace I leave with you; my peace I give you. I do not give to you as the world gives. Do not let your hearts be troubled and do not be afraid (John 14:27, NIV)*. Notice how Jesus emphasized the peace He left us by saying it is His peace. When Scripture emphasizes a word or phrase, we should take notice.

WHEN SCRIPTURE ITEMIZES

When the scripture lists items, it is a good indication for us that we have something to learn. In Proverbs 6:16-19 the Scripture makes a seven point list. As you read, number them in your Bible.

WHEN SCRIPTURE QUESTIONS

When the Bible asks questions, is it asking the question of you? In 1 Kings 18:21, Ahab asked the people, *How long will you waver between two opinions?* This verse becomes a powerful question for us to ask ourselves. How long will we waver? When will we trust God completely and totally?

WHEN SCRIPTURE BUILDS TO A CONCLUSION

In Titus chapter 2, Paul begins by talking to older men. From there he speaks to older women and then to younger women. Then he speaks to young men. After that he speaks to slaves and then to masters. Finally in verse 11, he gets to his main point which is that salvation is for all. No matter what age, gender, social status, or job description, God came to save us all. You might not see that conclusion if you weren't looking for how one scripture builds toward the next verse.

WHEN SCRIPTURE TEACHES

"And Saul was there, giving approval to his death. On that day a great persecution broke out against the church at Jerusalem, and all except the apostles were scattered throughout Judea and Samaria. Godly men buried Stephen and mourned deeply for him. But Saul began to destroy the church. Going from house to house, he dragged off men and women and put them in prison. Those who had been scattered preached the word wherever they went" (Acts 8:1-4 NIV).

At the time of Acts 8, there was great persecution against the church. The apostles and the people were scattered all over the known world. It was a terrible time for the people who were faithful to God. But even in these terrible events, we learn in verse 4 that those who had been scattered preached wherever they went and more people were saved.

God turned a bad thing to good. It is wonderful when we read scripture and learn such valuable truths about God. He turns bad to good. These kinds of lessons can only be learned if you are reading carefully with comprehension instead of reading large amounts of material and not understanding it.

READ THE BOOK

I once heard a preacher on television recite a poem about Bible reading. It is very simple and even a little funny, but it tells us exactly what we must do if we are going to experience God's presence in our daily quiet time. The poem reads like this:

READ THE BOOK

Verse One

Read the Book
Read the Book
Read the Book

Verse Two

Read the Book
Read the Book
Read the Book

Verse Three *(you can probably recite it by now)*
Read the Book
Read the Book
Read the Book

The Hebrews writer tells us about the power of God's Word:

"For the word of God is living and active. Sharper than any double-edged sword, it penetrates even to dividing soul and spirit, joints, and marrow; it judges the thoughts and attitudes of the heart" (Hebrews 4:12, NIV).

The Word of God reveals our hearts. It also reveals God to us. Most importantly, it offers real solutions to life's problems. The Book is alive! When you read a paragraph in the Bible, stop, go back, read it again. As you read, pick out important words or phrases. Learn real life lessons that will change your life. Read the Book.

REFLECTION

As you read the Scriptures, it is important that you take time to reflect on the words to determine the message God is giving you for today. Many times the same verses will give you different messages for different days because the Word of God is living, breathing, and active. His Word can penetrate your heart and give you hope no matter what situation you are facing.

Ask yourself some questions to determine what God is saying to you through His words.

What has happened to you in the last few months or days that has you perplexed, upset, or worried or has given you great joy, peace, or hope? Does this passage bring your situation to mind?

Have you prayed about it? Do your prayers seem to be reaching God or do you feel inadequate in your prayers? Does this verse give you any insight into the prayers you've been praying?

Is there an action that these verses instruct you to do? Does this action seem frightening or impossible? Can you confirm through prayer or other verses that God is telling you to act?

WRITE AS YOU READ

CHAPTER 4

*Write, therefore, what you have seen, what is now
and what will take place later.*
Revelation 1:19

I once heard Chuck Swindoll speak at a conference on biblical exposition. He said something I have never forgotten. He was speaking about writing while you read the Bible. He used this phrase: "Over the lips and through the finger tips."

Every time you and I read the Bible, we should have our pen in hand poised and ready to record facts, observations, insights, questions, and applications.

A small container with colored pencils, highlighters, pens, and pencils sits on the table next to my quiet-time place. As I read, I can mark places I find enlightening.

What a thrill it is to look through the pages of my Bible or one of my notebooks and find notes I have made during an intimate moment with the Lord. Frankly, the joy of that special fellowship comes back to me every time I read something I have written during my quiet time.

During our quiet time of intimate fellowship with the Lord, we allow Him to teach us. But because our quiet time is done on a regular daily basis, we are often unable to remember everything we've learned. Writing while we read is the best way to retain all the truth God teaches us during our quiet time. However, the lessons will do no good for us unless we can find what we have written. Suggestions in this chapter are for systematic projects we can do to keep all the insights at our fingertips.

WRITE A PERSONAL COMMENTARY

There are hundreds of commentaries available in Christian bookstores. Some are old classics and some are more modern. Some commentaries deal with original Greek and Hebrew meanings describing in full the nuances and significance of words. Others list references of complementary Scriptures or explain in detail the meanings of the verses.

Some commentaries are conservative and others are more radical. Some are collections of sermons by famous preachers who have systematically preached through the Bible verse-by-verse. Others provide practical advice.

Reading commentaries helps us to understand the context, the language structure, the historical significance, and background of the passages. In addition, when we read and meditate on scriptures, the Holy Spirit gives us valuable practical understanding and insights for our daily lives. As God reveals His heart to us, we can write a personal commentary on the verses of each chapter.

When I started my personal commentary, I was a young Christian. In fact, I was a teenager. I was not fully aware of many doctrines and teachings that might be found in the verses of the Bible. The nuances of language and deep insights were not apparent to me. However, I started my own commentary on the Gospel of John. I still have that little notebook. I often refer to it because of the unique insights God gave to me as a young teenage girl.

Today I have a more grown-up version of my personal commentary notebook with lots of scripture references and broader insights and questions.

It is amazing how many times I go to these two homemade commentaries when I am studying or preparing to teach or speak. They are resources of insights and understanding. I am amazed at how many times my teenaged version gives me fresh, vibrant insights I don't readily see as an adult.

No matter what I am doing—whether preparing a lesson or writing or simply reading—I find my personal commentary is valuable to me.

You can begin your personal commentary too. Start with a three-ring binder with blank pages and tab dividers. You may want to use a separate tab divider for each book of the Bible; however, in the beginning, you may want to start with an alphabetical index tab set. This will keep your notebook from being too crowded since there are only 26 alphabet tabs instead of 66 for the books of the Bible.

If you use alphabetical tabs, you would simply put all the Bible books behind their respective first letter. "J," for instance, would contain Joshua, Judges, Job, John, James, and Jude. Later, if your commentary gets too large, you may want to get individual tabs for each book. I have used the alphabetical system for years and it works well.

As you start your commentary begin with a blank page. On the top write the title of the book and the chapter number. Begin with verse one of the chapter.

After the number "1," record comments, facts, and information about verse one. Your comments may be personal in nature as you write what practical insight God has taught you in your reading of that verse. The comments you make in your personal commentary may be historical if you have read something significant in the margin notes or if you realize the verse relates to some other facts that you have studied.

Look at other verses listed in the margin or study notes of your Bible. As you read these related verses, you may find something interesting that you want to record in your personal commentary.

Note the context of the verse by reading the verses before and after. Who is the author? Who is the audience? What is the main emphasis? Are there other issues mentioned? As you answer these questions, your commentary will begin to take shape.

As you begin this commentary process, I don't recommend that you try to "take on" the whole Bible at once. To decide to write a commentary on the whole Bible is not a task even the most gifted and experienced scholars would attempt without a lot of help, perhaps even a team of scholars.

Instead of tackling the whole Bible, begin with one chapter of the Bible. You will not feel overwhelmed if you are working on one chapter at a time.

How do you write the commentary? Begin by answering some questions:

1) Who is the writer? Why do you think he wrote the book? What do you know about him? Who is he speaking to? For example, in the book of Hebrews, the writer is speaking to Jewish Christians. In the book of Romans, Paul is speaking to the believers at Rome. How does this cultural atmosphere affect what the writer is saying in the verses? If the verse is written to a certain category of people, how does it relate you?

2)   If the writer has written other books of the Bible, ask yourself whether he addressed the same issues in his other writings? How does it compare with the verses you are reading now? In Philippians, Paul talks about the armor of God. Does he mention weapons, armor, or battles anywhere else in his writings? Do they relate to this passage? Use the references in the margin of your Bible to find related scriptures or use a concordance to find additional verses on the subject.

3)   Does the verse fall into natural divisions? For example, 2 Corinthians 1:10: *He has delivered us…and he will deliver us.* These are two natural divisions—he has and he will. When writing your commentary on this verse you could reflect on how God has delivered His people throughout history and then how He has delivered you from situations throughout your life. Especially notice the emphasis on the fact that God has delivered us from certain death. How did God deliver us?Reflect on what that rescue means in the life on an individual believer. After you have explored the deliverance of God in the past, then contemplate the assurance of the future. Can you believe He will be your deliverer in the future based on His past performance and activity in your life? Write your reflections in your commentary.

4)   Does the verse contain a contrast? Do you see any comparisons in the verse? When you read a passage such as, *But we have this treasure in jars of clay to show that this all-surpassing power is from God and not from us,* [12] ask yourself, "What is the difference between jars of clay and treasures?"

Or in 2 Corinthians 6:8-10, "*…through glory and dishonor, bad report, and good report; genuine, yet regarded as impostors; known, yet regarded as unknown; dying and yet we live on; beaten, and yet not killed; sorrowful, yet always rejoicing; poor, yet making many rich; having nothing, and yet possessing everything*" (NIV)

Ask yourself the meaning of these opposites. Then elaborate on each of these contrasts in your commentary.

5) Is there a list in the verse? Write the list on your commentary pages and give the list a title to explain what the writer is teaching.

6) Look up word definitions and write them in your commentary.

7) As you read, look for exhortation, instructions, warnings, and facts. All of these will become part of your personal commentary.

The process of writing your personal commentary need not become overwhelming or burdensome. Let it become an extension of your learning process. Simply write as you read. Write a lot on one verse and just a sentence or a word on another. Don't be restricted by any space or artificial rules. If you use a spiral or loose-leaf notebook, you can write as much or as little as you like. Don't be concerned about your writing skills. It isn't the quality of the prose that matters; it is the quality of the message you have learned. Since that comes from God, as you are reading and spending your quiet time with Him, you don't have to worry about grammar and spelling.

Reading with understanding is discussed in detail in the chapter on reading. Now you should begin writing what you've learned. You will learn the meaning and application of each passage more fully if you write down what you observe and learn as you read.

WRITE YOUR PERSONAL TOPICAL BIBLE

My friend Kate [13] asked if she could talk to me privately. I listened as Kate described her problem. She was afraid—unrealistically. Afraid to leave her children, even with trusted friends. She couldn't relax. When attending a ladies conference, she feared her children might need her while she was away, even though they were with their loving and responsible father.

She was anxious about all kinds of potential physical terrors, yet she knew that her dread was actually a spiritual problem. She asked me to pray and to help. Clichés couldn't help Kate. I recognized pat answers would be empty and useless, but I knew scripture would comfort and teach her. Only the Word of God would be a true help. But how could I find scriptures that would restore health to Kate?

Fortunately, for several years I had been building a personal topical Bible. On this day it became a lifeline to help Kate. I turned to the "F" tab in my topical Bible notebook and found a page titled, "Fear." The page was filled with verses that explained God's power for times of fear. There were verses written in my notebook that declared the trustworthiness of God. Verses that proved God was faithful and could be relied upon. I was able to give Kate an arsenal of help for her problem.

Here is the letter I wrote to Kate:

> *Dear Kate,*
>
> *Thank you for sharing with me about your difficulties with fear. I feel so honored to be your friend. A powerful weapon to help you overcome your anxious feelings is at your disposal: the Word of God. It is a sword. When the fears come, you can take a swipe at them with your sword. You do this by memorizing verses for the battle. Here are some sword blades for you to use:*
>
> *When I am afraid, I will trust in you (Psalm 56:3).*
>
> *Fear not, for I have redeemed you; I have summoned you by name; you are mine (Isaiah 43:1b).*
>
> *From heaven the Lord looks down and sees all mankind; from his dwelling place he watches all who live on earth — he who forms the hearts of all, who considers everything they do (Psalm 33:13-15).*
>
> *For I am the Lord, your God, who takes hold of your right hand and says to you, Do not fear: I will help you (Isaiah 41:13).*
>
> *In you our fathers put their trust, they trusted and you delivered them (Psalm 22:4).*

I know that God will help you, Kate, as you trust in Him and put fear behind you. May you move forward in confidence.

Love, Karen

A TOPICAL BIBLE: COMFORT, ANSWERS, AND RESOURCES

Have you ever faced a problem and wished you could find a particular verse? A verse that would provide answers to your dilemma? Perhaps you remember reading a verse like that one time but you can't remember where the verse is located in the Bible. Making your own topical Bible will put all of these special verses at your fingertips.

If someone asks you to give a devotional or speak to a class or small group about a particular subject, you may wonder, "How will I find any information on the subject?" Your topical Bible will give you a great start.

A small loose-leaf notebook is my constant companion when I study the Bible. It contains my personal topical Bible. As I read through the Bible during my quiet time, I keep the notebook nearby. When I find a verse that helps me in some area of my life, I record it in my notebook.

The notebook is a valuable resource. When I am preparing a presentation and I need some Bible reference for clarification, I can turn to my notebook and find an appropriate verse. If someone calls me and asks me to speak at a meeting next week on the subject of God the Creator, I can turn to that section of my personal topical Bible and find several dozen verses to jump-start my preparation.

And I never have to wonder, "Where was that verse that I read the other day that meant so much to me?" because I can find it immediately in my personal topical Bible.

How to make your Personal Topical Bible Notebook

Materials needed:

- Loose-leaf binder. Mine is 8" x 5" for ease of handling; any size will do.
- Blank lined paper
- Alphabet divider pages
- Dividers with blank tabs

Place the alphabet divider pages in the binder first, then follow with the blank tabbed dividers. Place a few blank pages behind each alphabet tab and each blank tab.

Place one or two blank pages at the front of the notebook. On the top of the first page, write the title: "Index." Along the left side of the page, list the alphabet, leaving four or five lines between each letter of the alphabet. You may want to use a second page for the whole alphabet or you can make two columns on one page.

Getting Started – Alphabet Tabs

You are now ready to start your topical Bible. As you read the Bible every day, you will frequently read verses that emphasize an important topic. These are the verses you want to choose for your topical Bible.

J for Joy

For example, Psalm 19:8 says, *The precepts of the Lord are right, giving joy to the heart.* As you read the verse, you see that the words are about joy. Now turn the "J" divider in your topical Bible. Write "Joy" at the top of one of the blank pages and then write out the verse. Next, go to the front of your notebook to the index page and next to the letter J, write the word "Joy."

On another day, you may read Psalm 16:11, *You have made known to me the path of life; you will fill me with joy in your presence....* You can then go to the page "Joy" in your notebook and add it to the list of verses on joy.

As you continue to read and study the Scriptures, you will find verses that emphasize other topics. Add these to your notebook.

O for Obedience

For example, when you read Hebrews 5:8, *Although, he was a son, he learned obedience from what he suffered...,* title a blank page behind the "O" tab "Obedience." Then write the verse. Later you can add verses to this page such as Psalm 112:1b: ... *Blessed is the man who fears the Lord, who finds great delight in his commands.*

Later add Deuteronomy 6:25: *And if we are careful to obey all this law before the Lord our God, as he as commanded us, that will be our righteousness.*

All of these verses are related to obedience. Be sure to place the word "Obedience" next to "O" in your index.

Expanding to the Blank Tabs

Reserve the blank tabs at the end of the notebook for special expanded subjects. A good place to write verses and your thoughts about a subject is behind one of the blank tabs. If, for instance, you are beginning to realize the many wonderful ways of God has done. Record those on a page behind one of the blank tabs. Label the tab "Blessings from God." You can make your personal list of special blessings God has given. You may want to list your family, your home, your church, and your discipleship group.

You can also add specific verses that tell of God's great provisions. For example, Psalm 40:2-3 tells us that God has lifted us out of the slimy pit, out of mud and mire, He set our feet on a rock. Psalm 106:44-45 states that God takes note of His people's distress when He hears their cries and that because of His great love, He rescues. Psalm 54:4a declares, *surely God is my help....* Hebrews 9:11 advises that when Christ came as high priest, He entered the most holy place by His own blood, once and for all, to do away with sin by His sacrifice. What a thrill it is to turn to the "Blessings from God" tab in my topical Bible and be reminded of how much God loves me.

Special Words For Me

Another blank tab in my notebook is labeled "Special Words for Me." Sometimes when I am stressed or distressed, God reveals himself vividly in the words of a beautiful verse. If so, the verse is recorded behind this tab. Weeks later, when I read the verse again, the words comfort and guide my life once again.

One of my favorite verses in this section in my topical Bible is 1 Timothy 1:16: *...I was shown mercy so that in me, the worst of sinners, Christ Jesus might display his unlimited patience....* Every time I read these words from Paul I am amazed at God's mercy and patience. I love the description of His patience—it is unlimited. How often I need Him to be patient with me.

Psalms to Pray

One blank tab in my book is labeled "Psalms to Pray." On the pages behind the tab, I have written various psalms that lend themselves to being prayed back to God in praise, thanksgiving, adoration, and supplication. Verses such as the following:

> *Be my rock of refuge to which I can always go; give the command to save me for you are my rock and my fortress (Psalm 71:3).*

O Sovereign Lord, you are God! Your words are trustworthy and you have promised these good things to your servant (2 Samuel 7:28).

How great you are, O Sovereign Lord! There is no one like you and there is no God but you…(2 Samuel 7:22).

Quotes

Another tabbed section can be labeled "Quotes." In this section, write quotes, quips, and thoughts. This tabbed section becomes a stockpile of nuggets clearly and concisely expressing the truths of God. Examples from my notebook are encouraging and convicting:

- "The only reason for a mountaintop experience is so that we can take what we've learned to the valley."
- "Do people know more about Jesus simply because they know me?"
- "The brook would lose its song if the rocks were removed."
- "And though there are times when I've stepped out of His will, I've never been out of His care."

Other Blank Tabs

Other ideas for the blank tabs are 1) lyrics of love songs, 2) names of Jesus, or 3) testimonies of salvation found in the Bible.

Valuable Asset

Your personal topical Bible and notebook will quickly become one of your most valuable resources as you store the choice morsels from your daily feast on His Word and as you document the deep truths learned in your study of God's Word.

Although your index will contain your personal list of topics, some topic suggestions include:

A   Asking forgiveness

B   Baptism

         Blessings

C   Changed lives

         Children

D   Daily devotions

         Deacons/Wives

         Discipline

E   Evangelism

F   Fear

         Forgiveness

         Friends

G   God the Creator

         God's names

         God's glory

         God reveals Himself

         God speaks to us

         God's throne

         God, who watches and cares

         Get out of debt

H   Home

         Humility

I   In His time

J   Jesus – God and man

         Joy

K   Kindness

L   Love

         Living in God's presence

M   Mercy

         My path

         My position with God

N   Names of Jesus

O	Obedience
P	Peace
	Prayer
	Praying for others (intercessory prayer)
	Public praise
Q	Quenching the spirit
R	Restoring and forgiving
	Reaching others
	Righteousness
S	Seeking God
	Silence from God
	Singing
T	Trinity
	Trust (faith)
U	Unchangeable God
V	Victory
W	Wife
	Walking with God
	Waiting on the Lord
	Word of God

JOURNALING

Journaling has been a difficult task for me. In my home, I have dozens of beautiful journals most of which have one-third to one-half of the pages filled. The rest of the pages are blank. I felt like a failure when I stand before the shelf in my closet staring at all the journals, wondering what is wrong with me.

Many of my friends have faithfully kept beautifully bound journals in pretty handwriting. They seem to have this area of their lives all together. I have felt foolish about how many journals I have started and never finished.

As I have considered the journal process, I've realized I have had unrealistic expectations for myself in this area. I thought my journal must contain an entry for each day. But for some of us, everyday journaling may be an unrealistic goal. Instead of expecting myself to write every day, then failing to do it, I needed to understand that I probably will never be perfectly consistent in writing journals. Therefore, I must only expect myself to journal on those days when it seems to be right for me.

The key is to have the journal in my quiet time basket or box —marker in place at the next blank page—ready for me to write.

I've also felt that to do journaling right, I needed to write beautiful poetic sentences using picturesque words that would bring tears to the eyes of whomever read them hundreds of years from now. But I have learned that to successfully journal, all I need to do is write down some of the events of my day or my week and write some of my feelings about those events. For example, after taking a couple of days off from work recently and taking a short trip to visit our son and daughter-in-law and our six-month-old granddaughter, Ashton, I wrote the trip in my journal.

I feel so much better about the journaling process since I've learned not to make the process a burden. I've learned I can write as often or as infrequently as I want to. I can write as little or as much as I want to on a given day. Not only that, I can write about the happenings of my life as well as the feelings and emotions of my life. Just these few conclusions have been a relief to me and have freed me to become more proficient at journaling.

Maybe you have set some unrealistic goals or expectations as well. If so, try to analyze why you haven't been successful and then decide whether your limitations or expectations are worthwhile.

In journaling class, the teacher said, "Write often; write fast; write everything!" This is good advice. If you do not let your journal get advantage over you, you will find that writing in your journal is a blessing. As you become proficient, you may want to write more and more.

In addition, I discovered that the journals that I had were not user-friendly. If I had ever written something profound or beautiful, I probably would never be able to find it again. I realized that I needed to find a way to index the references I had written.

In the instructions below, I have given you some ideas to help catalog and index your journal.

How to get started

Buy a notebook, preferably one with fixed pages instead of the loose-leafed ringed binder type. Your journal notebook can be as simple as a spiral-bound pad or as elaborate as a cloth-bound or leather-bound hardback book with blank pages. On the first page of the journal put the date on the day you begin writing in the journal. When you have finished all the pages, return to the first page and record the date of the last entry as well. When you refer to this journal in the future, you will be happy to be able to pinpoint the dates of the entries.

For me, writing only on one side of the page of the journal is helpful in keeping a neat appearance. I have become discouraged in the past, because about halfway through the journal, the whole look of the journal begins to get messy. One of the ways to eliminate this tattered look is to write only on the front side of each page. In addition, having a blank page opposite each page allows me to add small notes, scriptures, drawings or stickers about the content of the opposite page.

As your write, number each page at the bottom. At the back of the journal, use a paper clip to clip off a section of five to ten pages to use as an index. Do not number these pages. As you write your journal, you will make entries about special events or feelings that are especially important and you know that you may want to go back to these entries at a later time. If so, record a title of that special entry in the index. Record the page number beside the index entry. You will then be able to scan the index in the future and know where to look for special entries.

The day after my daughter's wedding, I wrote a few pages in my journal about the events and the blessings of the day. In the index of that journal, I wrote, "Thoughts on Cherry's Wedding, page 28." At any time, I can easily find those thoughts by going to the index. This indexing technique is especially helpful if you write in your journal about a certain scripture verse. Write the verse in the index so you can retrieve your thoughts.

When I think of my life experiences, I regret so often that I did not keep a journal or diary of past events. There are many things that have happened to me that I thought I would never forget. Sadly, I have forgotten them. If I had written all those events in a journal, I would be so happy to read about them now. I have resolved not to let anymore events pass without recording them in a journal.

WRITE YOUR OWN DICTIONARY

I have had the privilege during the past couple of years to help a friend begin his spiritual journey. When we first began talking about spiritual matters, I realized quickly that he and I didn't have the same vocabulary. He had little experience in religion and had never read the Bible. He knew little of the words, phrases, and terminology of my Christian world. I used a language that could be called Christianese and he couldn't relate to the words I was using. I often used a term that caused him to ask for a definition.

After several frustrating conversations, I decided to build a personal dictionary that would include not only definitions of important words from the Bible but also of the Christianese words that had become such a big part of my common speech.

There is great value in putting down a precise definition and description of familiar words. We think we know what faith is, but until we have to define the word in a concise, well-written sentence, we may not have full understanding of what it means. We think we understand

83

concepts like baptism or communion, but writing a description of these ordinances will give us greater insight into what we really believe about them.

Here are some of the Christianese words and phrases that could be included in your personal dictionary:

Lead in prayer
Atonement
Sacrifice
Angels
Demons
Follow the Lord
Scriptural baptism
Season of prayer
Quiet time

There is often a great difference between the popular definition of a word and how God defines it. I often hear someone on the TV news say, "We can get through this tragedy because we have a lot of faith," or someone will say, "Keep the faith." These are common statements, which seem on the surface to say that someone is trusting in God to handle the situations of their lives. But most people who say these words are not considering God at all. Most are having "faith" in themselves, or in fate, or in nature.

Sometimes it seems like the faith of our popular culture is only faith in faith. Most don't understand that faith is being "certain of what you hope for and certain of what you do not see" as it is defined in Hebrews 11:1. Real faith knows there is a God even though we cannot see Him. Real faith knows God is the creator and sustainer of life. Real faith is trusting that God will fulfill every promise He has made. Real faith is being certain that no matter what situation we face in life, He is in control.

It is so easy to get caught in the world's view and definition of phrases. Preparing our personal dictionary helps us understand certain important terms. In making a precise definition, we learn what we truly believe.

Making a personal dictionary is very simple. Use a plain notebook—label the pages with the letters of the alphabet. Record the word and definition in the appropriate letter section. Use simple language. Write clear, concise sentences. Add scripture verses to verify your definition.

WRITE YOUR BELIEFS

As I began to study the Bible and have more and longer quiet times with Him and as I attended Bible study classes, heard sermons, and participated in discussions, I formulated certain understandings of God and His relationship with humankind.

These understandings are the basic tenets of my belief statement.

The exercise of writing down our beliefs will cause us to begin to understand God and to become sure of our stance on any subject. I made a notebook called "My Personal Statement of Faith." Not only have I written the facts down about what I believe, but in doing so, I have considered all the facts, weighed them against scripture, and formulated my position.

Your personal belief statement will probably take some time to develop. Being sure of what you believe is a result of weeks, months, and years of study. Use the following suggested topics to help you write down your beliefs about each subject:

1)   What do you believe about creation? Did God create the world? How? When? What about evolution?

2)   What do you believe about God? How many gods are there? Where is He? What does He do? What is His nature?

3)   What do you believe about the Trinity? How do you explain this phenomenon?

85

4) What do you believe about Jesus? Where did He come from? What did He do on earth? What does His death mean? Where is He now?

5) What do you believe about the Holy Spirit? Who is He? What is His function? Where is He? How do you get to know Him?

6) What do you believe about a personal relationship with God? Is it possible to know God intimately? What does He do in your life? Can you depend on Him?

7) What do you believe about the church? Who is the church? What is the purpose of the church?

8) What do you believe about heaven? Is it real? Where is it? How do you get there?

9) What do you believe about hell? Is it real? Where is it? How do you avoid going there?

10) What is prayer? What is worship?

11) What do you believe about the Bible? Who wrote it? What is its purpose?

There are numerous other subjects about which you can formulate a belief statement—missions, stewardship, the return of Jesus. When you have thought through a topic carefully and researched the scriptures for verification, record it on your belief list.

Be sure to write the belief statements in clear language. It is better to be positive in your statement rather than negative. Don't write why what someone else believes is wrong. Instead write what you believe and why. Be sure to include scripture references for each belief. In this way, you will see that you have a scriptural reason for each belief.

As you write your personal doctrinal statement, you may be surprised at some things you believe that you didn't think about before or you may even be surprised that as you try to put a belief into words, you were wrong and it is not validated in scripture.

Writing your personal belief statement is a great exercise for your quiet time, and your spiritual growth and understanding as well.

WRITE YOUR PERSONAL MISSION STATEMENT

A friend of mine encouraged me to write a mission statement for my life. I wasn't so sure that I could do it or that I needed to do it. A mission statement sounded like something a committee would do before embarking on some important project. However, the more I thought of it, the more I realized that without a clear, concise statement of my goals, intentions, aspirations, and expectations, I would be wandering through life hoping that something would happen that would motivate, stimulate, or encourage me.

A carefully constructed personal mission statement will give direction and meaning to every event in your life. When someone asks you to take on a new project, you can evaluate it against your mission statement. If it fits well, it will help you accomplish your goals. If it doesn't, you can turn it down because it doesn't fit.

How to write your statement

Begin with a few verbs. Choose the verbs that describe your life's aims and desires. Add descriptions of what you want your life to represent or accomplish.

When I wrote my mission statement, I had many false starts. I tried to think of what was important to me and what I wanted to "do with my life." I had so many thoughts that it was like a rain shower of information. I knew I needed to narrow it down to the most important areas.

One morning I was reading 1 Thessalonians chapter two and God stopped me at verse 11.

> For you know that we dealt with each of you as a father deals with his own children, encouraging, comforting, and urging you to live lives worthy of God, who calls you into his kingdom and glory. And we also thank God continually because, when you received the word of God, which you heard from us, you accepted it not as the word of men, but as it actually is, the Word of God, which is at work in you who believe (1 Thessalonians 2:11-13, NIV).

87

When I saw those three verbs—encouraging, comforting, and urging—I realized those were the three verbs that would best state my mission statement. As you can see in my mission statement below, I used a lot of Paul's words in trying to express what I believe God wants me to do with the rest of my life.

My mission statement:

Delighting to share through writing and speaking not only the gospel of Christ but my life as well.
To ENCOURAGE others to know the Lord through the Word of God,
To COMFORT those who are hurting,
To URGE everyone I meet to live a life of excellence.
Teaching others to receive the Word of God not as the word of men but as it actually is: the Word of God.

Using Paul's verbs, I have expressed my desire to use writing and speaking to reach others with God's message of salvation, encouragement, and comfort as well as emphasizing that each of us can live an excellent life.

Shortening the mission statement even further, I can say, "Through writing and speaking, I share the gospel and my life by encouraging, comforting and urging excellent living through Christ."

If you have a purpose that you have set clearly in your mind, your life will be dedicated to reaching those goals and aspirations. If you don't, you may never accomplish anything. A mission statement will help direct every move closer to your goals.

As I read my mission statement and consider my life's activities, I realize that there are some things I should do and some I shouldn't. There are some projects that come along that I need to say, "No that isn't for me," even though it may be a worthwhile or enjoyable project. It doesn't fit my mission statement.

Write your mission statement. The best way to get started is to make a short list of the three or four most important things that you want to do or feel called to do. Then beside each item on your list, write down a verb that best describes this activity. After you have chosen your verbs, write a clear, short sentence that fully defines what you want to do with your life.

You might want to start by making two different mission statements: one for your personal life including your goals and aspirations for your job, family, and self, and the second for your ministry. Later you may want to combine them into one mission statement that incorporates all aspects of your life.

Defining your mission statement may take some time, so do not get discouraged.

SHORT TITLES OF BIBLE CHAPTERS

One of the most interesting ways to work through your Bible reading during your quiet time is to give each chapter of the Bible a title. If you read a chapter that contains many verses, coming up with a chapter title will make you think through all you have read and identify the major theme or themes of the verses as well as categorize the theme in importance.

When you identify the theme or themes, you will be amazed at two things that will happen. First, you will more fully understand the chapter because you have analyzed it so carefully. Secondly, you will remember the contents of the chapter much longer and you may never forget some of the lessons you've identified. A bonus benefit of this exercise is that you will begin to identify principles that you can trace through other Scripture passages.

After you become proficient at making chapter titles, you can enhance your learning experience by trying the following exercise. Try keeping your titles down to five words or less. Doing this is a tough exercise and requires a lot of thought and practice, but the reward is incredible. Real understanding is required if you are going to boil down all the facts, lessons, or truths in a number of verses to no more than five words.

NOTES TO YOURSELF

As I read along during my quiet time each day, I am often so amazed at how relevant the verses are to my current situation.

When I am feeling depressed, the verses that stand out during my reading are verses of encouragement and hope. If I am worried about finances, my passage for the day will inevitably be about God's care and provision. If I am full of joy, the verses will always reflect the great joy we have in Jesus.

Because these verses mean so much to me, I want to try to remember them during the day. I decided to keep the verses before me by writing them on a 3x5 card to take with me during the day. At the top of the card, I write the phrase "God's Words to Karen." I put this personalized message on my mirror so I can read it while I am dressing and later on my computer stand and later on the refrigerator door to remind me of the special message God spoke to me.

I often take the card to work with me and put it on my desk so I can be reminded. I purchased some pretty note cards and copied the verse on the card so it gets the attention of others in my office. The cards have become a daily novelty in the office.

STUDY PLACES

As you are reading in your daily quiet time, you will notice the names of places. Often one place may be mentioned many times in the Bible, sometimes in both the Old and New Testaments. If you try to learn as much as you can about these places, you will often find hidden truths.

When you come across the name of a place in your reading, look up that name in a concordance. Then read all the verses about that place and find everything that ever happened there.

If you read about Bethel in the Old Testament, you find that Jacob went to that place over and over again, and he met God there each time. Recording these events in your notebook will help you understand how God dealt with this man who would eventually father the nation of Israel. It is a beautiful and rewarding study.

In 2 Kings 6, there is a place called Dothan. In that chapter, Elisha and his servant are in big trouble while in the city of Dothan. Their enemies surround them but angels in chariots of fire rescue them. When I read of that event, I wondered if anything else had ever happened at Dothan. I discovered the place is mentioned only in one other place in the Bible. That is in Genesis 37. Joseph got into big trouble at Dothan too, but instead of an army of angels, he was thrown into a pit, sold into slavery, came to great harm and sorrow as he was abandoned by his brothers. But in God's time, Joseph was greatly used of God.

So, two events happened in Dothan. In one event, God sent angels to rescue Elisha and in the other event Joseph was captured and sold. What kind of a conclusion can I draw from those two events? The answer is that our lives are a little like Dothan. We get into trouble too. Sometimes God may deliver us quickly, swiftly, and miraculously like Elisha or He may let us go through trouble and sorrow like Joseph. Either way, God is in control of the situation.

OTHER CREATIVE TECHNIQUES

Word Study

Words are great. I love words. I love to see the combinations of words that creative writers come up with. I love the emotions words can generate. I love the pictures words can draw. For a creative and interesting insight into Scripture, look up a word. Try to find out how many ways it is used in Scripture.

Singing

Don't say you can't sing, because God hears your heart not your voice. So sing, sing, sing, sing, sing in your quiet time.

Pick out a few of your favorite hymns and choruses. Write them in your notebook. Change all the lyrics to personal pronouns like me, I, you etc. For example, I change the lyrics of "In His Presence" to "In Your presence, there is comfort; in Your presence there is peace." This personalization helps the song touch my heart. In the song "He is Lord," I change the wording to "You are Lord."

The beautiful and poetic lyrics of songs can touch you emotionally and spiritually.

Other Techniques

Many other techniques will enhance your quiet time. Use some of the ideas in the list below to develop your quiet time even more.

- Give a title to every Psalm
- Memorize
- Condense chapters to five words
- Outline chapters
- Outline books
- Write poetry
- Write original Psalms
- Worship
- Make up motions to songs
- Sit on the porch to read
- Put a Bible program on your mp3 player and let it read to you

PRAYER

CHAPTER 5

Be joyful always; pray continually; give thanks in all circumstances
1 Thessalonians 5:17-18

...the Lord our God is near us whenever we pray to him.
Deuteronomy 4:7 b

As I stood in the entrance to the ballroom of the Sheraton Astrodome Hotel, I wondered why I was there. The evening traffic and blaring news reports of flooded streets and dangerous intersections agitated my nerves in the hour-plus drive I'd just taken to get to the hotel. I looked down at my soaked shoes and wet clothes. My umbrella had failed to protect me from the storm.

Music from the Prayer and Fasting Gathering filled my ears. I didn't know anyone in the room. I wondered again, "Why had I come?" I started to leave but felt the room pulling me in.

I found an empty seat in one of the hundreds of circles of chairs and smiled at those already seated. After some instruction from the speakers, my circle gathered closely and began to pray.

Here I was, soaking wet and huddled with strangers, yet we were now clinging together in prayer. As the prayers rose to heaven, gentle warmth came over me that replaced my cold, wet mood. No longer alone, I felt a kinship with my group. Instead of nerves on edge, my heart became calm. Though the storm raged outside, peace reigned inside. All because of prayer.

Prayer is the ultimate joy for Christians. It is our communion with God. It is our bridge into His presence. Our opportunity to share intimately with the creator of the universe.

No quiet time is complete without prayer.

JESUS PRAYED

Jesus understood the importance of prayer. One exhausting week, He showed how important prayer is. He had walked for miles with his four handpicked key leaders. When the five of them arrived at Peter and Andrew's house, they expected to eat a good meal and rest. But no fires burned and no food aromas filled the air because Peter's mother-in-law was ill. Jesus' gentle touch healed her.

Then friends, neighbors, even strangers crowded into the tiny house bringing the sick and demon possessed. Jesus touched broken and twisted limbs with healing power. He spoke over blind eyes and deaf ears giving sight and hearing. He sent demons out of the door as freedom entered trapped souls.

When the commotion died down, Jesus and His disciples finally rested with the deep sleep that comes from exhaustion.

But Jesus didn't sleep long.

Very early in the morning, while it was still dark, Jesus got up, left the house and went off to a solitary place, where he prayed (Mark 1:35).

In the dark, He made His way to a place where no one would see Him—a secluded, quiet, solitary place. And there He prayed.

At age 30, Jesus had begun making public appearances. John baptized Him. The Father acknowledged and commissioned Him. And now crowds followed Him everywhere to see power and capabilities. Every moment of His life was now busy. But early that morning, He knew where He wanted to go. To the Father. Finding a solitary place, He prayed.

I've often wondered how Jesus prayed early that morning. Since Jesus was one hundred percent human as well as fully God, His prayers may have taken on human voice.

- Perhaps He prayed for direction—asking to know the Father's way instead of the way that seemed best to the crowds.
- Perhaps He prayed for focus—asking the Father to keep His attention on the plan of redemption and off the excitement of the crowds.
- Perhaps He prayed for power—asking the Father to give power over the many problems on earth.
- Perhaps He prayed for strength—for He needed stamina to walk the miles and to deal with the crowds.
- Perhaps He prayed for wisdom—knowing what lay ahead. He knew how much opposition was coming. He knew He needed to be wise in each encounter.

More likely, He spent those early morning hours in loving conversation with His Father. Jesus may have described all the events of the day…the people gathering around Peter's door, Peter's mother-in-law, her illness, and her joy at being made well. Perhaps He spoke of the disease and demons in the crowd. And the Father may have said, "I know, I saw."

As the Father comforted and encouraged Jesus, perhaps He reminded Jesus of the future. Together they may have recounted the plan that had been in place since the beginning—the glorious plan that would graciously bring the lost and dying world back from rebellion.

What a prayer time on that early morning! Fervent prayer on the eve of the three years that would change the world forever.

I've been in prayer meetings where prayer huddles joined hands and voices. I've heard petitions placed before the Lord. I've participated in praise services when everyone in the room was worshiping the Father. I've spent time on my knees alone with God when He was so real and present with me that I felt I actually touched Him. But nothing compares to that early morning in a solitary place when Jesus slipped away to speak to the Father.

Nothing keeps me, however, from continuing to reach for that kind of intimacy. Every time I spend an hour on my face before God, I receive a small glimpse of the kind of communication Jesus had with the Father.

PRAYER: OUR PRIMARY FOCUS

When I was a young girl, our church held a weeklong revival meeting. My mother invited the preachers for lunch at our home. As we sat down around that table that day, my daddy asked the visiting preacher to pray. I don't remember the words he said, but I do remember, even all these years later, how personal and intimate the conversation was. When he prayed, Rev. Charles McCamey was speaking with someone he knew. I determined in my heart, as a little child, that someday, I would know God that way too.

A child prays, "God is great, God is good. Let us thank Him for our food." An older adult prays, "Father, You are so real to me today and I welcome You into my home." Both are prayers of intimacy.

The child prays to a God whom she knows as good and full of love. The grandmother prays with great wisdom, knowing that God is not only good and loving, but most of all faithful. Intimacy knows God is present and that even when we can't see Him, God is still holy, loving, and faithful.

Prayer is the primary focus of a Christian's life. Prayer is the communication between God and us. To defeat the devil, comfort the heart, awaken the soul, reveal God, and change our life, we must utilize part of our daily quiet time in rich prayer.

PRAYER IS A DIALOGUE

Think of prayer as contact with God. An opportunity to touch God or make a connection with Him. Just as a telephone call allows transmissions from both ends of the line, prayer is a dialogue.

We don't simply tell Him our thoughts, feelings, and ideas or notify Him of our plans; we participate in an interchange discussion with God. Prayer is sincerely taking a look at God's plans, not only our plan.

He is pleased when we express ourselves. He is thrilled when we take time to hear from Him too. He is delighted when we respond to Him with, "Your will, not mine."

It may help you to think of prayer as a dialogue, a reciprocation between the Father and you. Prayer is a time of telling God about your hopes, dreams, and wants. It is also time to hear His hopes, dreams, and desires for you. When you take time to hear Him, you will discover His plans are always bigger than yours are. He is dreaming brighter, hoping higher, and wanting better for you in every situation.

Our responsibility in prayer is to learn the give and take of communion with Him. As we do, our two wills will become a union.

There is a popular business term called "synergy." It means that two companies with different products may have similar operations or services which can be combined on certain tracks for the benefit of both companies. But don't confuse synergy with prayer. Prayer is more than synergy. It is intimacy. Intimacy with God is more than familiarity or similar tracks. It is an alliance of wills. When my will becomes a shadow of the will of God, I have reached a deep relationship with Him called intimacy.

How can we find this kind of intimate praying during our daily quiet time? The following practical ideas will add depth to your daily quiet time.

PRAYING ON YOUR KNEES

I have never discovered anything that ushers me into the presence of God like getting on my knees. The simple act of moving to my knees before Him is an amazing phenomenon.

Throughout the scriptures, men and women knelt and fell on their faces before God. When Solomon dedicated the temple, he knelt on the platform before the whole congregation. Can you imagine the scene? The great King of Israel humbling himself before God and raising his hands to heaven.

> "For Solomon had made a bronze platform five cubits long, five cubits wide, and three cubits high, and had set it in the midst of the court; and he stood on it, knelt down on his knees before all the assembly of Israel, and spread out his hand toward heaven" (2 Chronicles 16:13 NKJV).

Daniel, the government official who loved God more than his lofty position, spent his quiet time on his knees. It was his habit from childhood. When wicked men turned up the heat of persecution, his response was to kneel before God.

"Now when Daniel knew that the writing was signed, he went home. And in his upper room, with his windows open toward Jerusalem, he knelt down on his knees three times that day, and prayed and gave thanks before his God, as was his custom since early days" (Daniel 6:10 NKJV).

Jesus himself knew the value of a position of humility before God. "And he was withdrawn from them about a stone's throw, and He knelt down and prayed" (Luke 22:41 NKJV). Stephen recognized his approaching death and yet he responded by kneeling before the Father. "Then he knelt down and cried out with a loud voice, 'Lord, do not charge them with this sin.' And when he had said this, he fell asleep" (Acts 7:60 NKJV).When Peter needed power for ministry, he knelt. "But Peter put them all out, and knelt down and prayed. And turning to the body he said, "Tabitha, arise." And she opened her eyes and when she saw Peter she sat up" (Acts 9:40 NKJV).

When Paul left the mission field, he prayed with the people he was leaving behind. He knelt to pray.

"And when he had said these things, he knelt down and prayed with them all" (Acts 20:36 NKJV).

During his journey back to Jerusalem and certain imprisonment, Paul knelt to pray.

"But when our time was up, we left and continued on our way. All the disciples and their wives and children accompanied us out of the city, and there on the beach we knelt to pray" (Acts 21:5 NIV).

David pleads with us to worship God on our knees.
"Come, let us bow down in worship, let us kneel before the Lord our Maker" (Psalm 95:6 NIV).

When Paul interceded for the church at Ephesus, he came to the Father kneeling.

"For this reason I kneel before the Father" (Ephesians 3:14 NIV).

Overwhelmed by the glory of God, Moses and Aaron fell facedown before him.

"Moses and Aaron went from the assembly to the entrance to the tent of meeting and fell facedown, and the glory of the Lord appeared to them" (Numbers 20:6 NIV).

Moses once spent 40 days on his face before God as he prayed for Israel.

"Then once again I fell prostrate before the Lord for forty days and forty nights; I ate no bread and drank no water, because of all the sin you had committed, doing what was evil in the Lord's sight and so provoking him to anger" (Deuteronomy 9:18 NIV).

When conviction for sins overwhelmed Ezra, he knelt.
"Then, at the evening sacrifice, I rose from my self-abasement, with my tunic and cloak torn, and fell on my knees with my hands spread out to the Lord my God and prayed: "O my God, I am too ashamed and disgraced to lift up my face to you, my God, because our sins are higher than our heads and our guilt has reached to the heavens" (Ezra 9:5-6 NIV).

Even demons and evil spirits fell before Jesus.
"Whenever the evil spirits saw him, they fell down before him and cried out, "You are the Son of God" (Mark 3:11 NIV).

Men and women in need came to Jesus in total humility. Jairus, the woman with the blood disease, and the Phoenician woman all fell at Jesus' feet.

"Then one of the synagogue rulers, named Jairus, came there. Seeing Jesus, he fell at his feet and pleaded earnestly with him, "My little daughter is dying. Please come and put your hands on her so that she will be healed and live" (Mark 5:22-23 NIV).

"Then the woman, knowing what had happened to her, came and fell at his feet and, trembling with fear, told him the whole truth" (Mark 5:33-34 NIV).

"In fact, as soon as she heard about him, a woman whose little daughter was possessed by an evil spirit came and fell at his feet. The woman was a Greek, born in Syrian Phoenicia. She begged Jesus to drive the demon out of her daughter" (Mark 7:25-26 NIV).

Those seeking salvation fell before him.
"As Jesus started on his way, a man ran up to him and fell on his knees before him. 'Good teacher,' he asked, 'what must I do to inherit eternal life?'" (Mark 10:17 NIV).

Those who were ill or who were in desperate trouble knelt before Jesus.

"While Jesus was in one of the towns, a man came along who was covered with leprosy. When he saw Jesus, he fell with his face to the ground and begged him, 'Lord, if you are willing, you can make me clean'" (Luke 5:12 NIV).

"When Mary reached the place where Jesus was and saw him, she fell at his feet and said, 'Lord, if you had been here, my brother would not have died'" (John 11:32 NIV).

When confronted by a Holy God, even wicked men fell to the ground.

"As he neared Damascus on his journey, suddenly a light from heaven flashed around him. He fell to the ground and heard a voice say to him, 'Saul, Saul, why do you persecute me?'" (Acts 9:3-4 NIV).

John saw the future when every creature will fall down kneeling in worship of God Almighty.

"When I saw him, I fell at his feet as though dead. Then he placed his right hand on me and said: 'Do not be afraid. I am the First and the Last. I am the Living One; I was dead, and behold I am alive forever and ever! And I hold the keys of death and Hades'" (Revelation 1:17-18 NIV).

"And when he had taken it, the four living creatures and the twenty-four elders fell down before the Lamb. Each one had a harp and they were holding golden bowls full of incense, which are the prayers of the saints" (Revelation 5:8 NIV).

"All the angels were standing around the throne and around the elders and the four living creatures. They fell down on their faces before the throne and worshiped God" (Revelation 7:11 NIV).

A position of humility before God is the best place to start your prayer life. Whether you are feeling great with everything going your way or whether you are in desperate trouble because of illness or sin, approach Him in a humbled position as you kneel before Him.

I like to get on my knees facing my sofa with my head on the cushion. It is a comfortable position for long periods of time. I also have a small stool about 12 inches high that allows me to rest my arms as I fall before Him. The sofa and the stool give me physical stability and comfort so that I don't get sidetracked by any physical discomfort. Instead I am able to give complete focus to God. You may try kneeling on a small pillow to protect your knees.

If you have a disability or have difficulty getting on your knees, try lying on your stomach or placing your head in your hands to put yourself physically in a humble position before Him. When Moses stood before God at the burning bush, God said, "Take off your shoes." It was an action of reverence and honor. If you can't physically maneuver to a kneeling or prostrate position, then take off your shoes. It's hard to feel pride when your feet are bare.

Obviously, a special physical position is not required to have an intimate time of prayer and communication with God, but if possible, kneel or bow. Your prayers will change dramatically. God will recognize your reverence and honor. He will reach to you with His loving touch. Your attitude will be different if you consciously and physically humble yourself before Him. You will be more likely to hear His words than to be demanding your own way.

INTERCESSORY PRAYER

After receiving the Ten Commandments, Moses came down out of Mt. Sinai to discover the people of Israel building a golden calf idol. In rebellion, they lost their trust in the power of Jehovah. Moses was shocked. God was angry. He prepared to destroy them completely.

What Moses did next is one of our best biblical examples of intercessory prayer. We can use the model of Moses to learn to intercede in prayer for those around us. We find his example in Deuteronomy.

First Moses fell down. Moses approached God in a totally humble position. He displayed no personal agenda.

"I lay prostrate before the Lord those forty days and forty nights because the Lord had said he would destroy you" (Deuteronomy 9:25 NIV).

Second, Moses recognized God as the sovereign Lord of all creation.

"I prayed to the Lord and said, 'O Sovereign Lord….'" (Deuteronomy 9:26a)

As Moses recognized God's power over all things, he clearly knew that God had the power to intercede in the lives of the people of Israel.

These two factors—humility and recognition of God's power —are the basis of all intercessory prayer. When we approach God in a contrite and humble spirit, recognizing that it is His power and His power alone that will make a difference, we are ready to begin to pray for others.

The people of Israel flagrantly sinned and failed to trust God. Moses did not deny it. In fact, he agreed God had every right to judge them harshly. He offered no excuse. He simply acknowledged the grievous sin. When we intercede, we must also honestly acknowledge failures and mistakes and call sin by its name.

Then Moses boldly prayed for the people. He recalled that God had redeemed them. He observed that these people were God's own possession. Then he reminded God of the covenant between them. Moses affirmed his belief in God's covenant.

> "'...do not destroy your people, your own inheritance that you redeemed by your great power and brought out of Egypt with a mighty hand. Remember your servants Abraham, Isaac and Jacob. Overlook the stubbornness of this people, their wickedness and their sin'" (Deuteronomy 9:26b-27 NIV).

Finally Moses considered God's reputation.

> "Otherwise, the country from which you brought us will say, 'Because the Lord was not able to take them into the land he had promised them, and because he hated them, he brought them out to put them to death in the desert'" (Deuteronomy 9:28 NIV).

Moses asked God to spare Israel because 1) they were redeemed, 2) they were God's possession, 3) God had a covenant with them, and 4) God's reputation was at stake.

Moses' bold prayer approach to God was personal and pointed. He was sure of his relationship with God and God's power. Not only that, he knew the merciful nature of God.

We can incorporate Moses' technique into our intercessory prayers too. For example, if someone you love is rebelling against God, you can intercede with Moses' approach.

1) Agree with God that your loved one is wrong in his or her actions.

2) Agree with God that your loved one deserves punishment for his or her actions.

3) Remind God that He is the God of true mercy and that He has promised redemption.

105

4)   Ask God to spare your loved one the punishment he or she deserves because of His mercy and His promises.

For example, you might intercede for your child in this way:

"Lord, my son is not behaving like a Christian. In fact, Lord, he is breaking my heart. I know that his actions hurt you too. He deserves your judgment.

But Lord, my son is your child. He belongs to you. Lord, you've promised that your seed will always return to you. I ask you Lord to bring my son home to you. I ask you to keep your promise. Lord, you are getting no glory from his life now. When you bring him back to you, we will give you all the glory."

In the case of illness, your intercessory prayer might sound like this:

"Lord, my sister is ill. I know how serious the illness is. I understand the consequences of it. I know the world is full of evil including sickness and death. But Lord, my sister is your child and your creation. She accepted you as her Savior when she was 12 years old. She loves you and serves you every day. You have blessed her in many ways. Lord, you've promised abundant life for your children. You promised healing in your name and I am asking you to heal her. Lord, the healing cannot happen without you. If you heal her, the world cannot say the doctors or medical science accomplished the healing. If you heal her, we will know that you alone did the healing. Lord, you will receive all the glory."

Intercessory prayer is especially appropriate when praying for salvation:

"Lord, my friend is lost and is not your child. He deserves death and punishment for his sins just like I do. But you, Lord, are full of compassion and mercy and not willing that any should perish. Bring my friend to the point of salvation. Lord, you've said that you will draw all men until you. I pray that you will draw him to you now. Lord, this salvation will bring you great glory and honor."

Intercessory prayers 1) recognize the problem, 2) acknowledge the seriousness of it, 3) remember the promises of God and the integrity of His character, and 4) boldly ask for His intervention.

Revolutionize your prayer life by acknowledging the seriousness of sin yet firmly placing it into the hands of God.

As we learn to pray like Moses, we will also learn to wait on the answer like Moses did. The Lord may move swiftly or He may move slowly. He may answer yes, no, or wait, but if you don't pray, He may not have a reason to intervene. He may act only according to His righteous nature in judgment instead of in His merciful nature—if you don't pray. If Moses had just agreed with God and given up on these people, God would have destroyed them. It certainly was God's right and prerogative to do it. But when Moses prayed an intercessory prayer, God changed His mind.

Can you persuade God? Yes. You can because He loves you as His child and He delights in answering your prayers.

To properly pray an intercessory prayer, follow these steps:

1)   Get prepared.
- Get to know God face-to-face through Bible reading and study.
- Live obediently to His commands.
- Spend daily time in prayer.
- Fast periodically.

2) Do whatever you can.
   - Just as Moses descended that mountain to first try to stop the rebellion, you must also give assistance to those in need.
   - Do whatever you can to help physically or financially.
   - Recommend professional help when needed.

3) Be humble before Him.
   - Get on your face before Him.
   - Fast.
   - Pray.
   - Search for Him.
   - Recognize His Lordship.

4) Be honest and direct
   - Acknowledge that sin is serious.
   - Acknowledge your limitations.
   - Acknowledge God's right to judge.

5) Be bold enough to ask
   - Ask God to change His mind.
   - Ask for God's mercy.
   - Ask for God's grace.
   - Ask for God's compassion.
   - Remind God of His promises.

Remember God may act only according to His righteous nature instead of His compassionate and merciful nature if you don't pray. Our intercessory prayers will reach the heart of God.

PRAYING THE PSALMS

Another way to bring new life and vigor to your prayers is to let God's words become your words by praying Scripture. His words are holy, pure, and true. What better words to use than God's own words? The Psalms is a perfect place to start this practice. Go through the Psalms and choose some prayers that David and other psalmists prayed. Write them into your notebook. Change the pronouns and verb tenses to make them relevant to you praying to God.

Begin your prayer time by praying these verses to God

"In the morning, O Lord, you hear my voice; in the morning I lay my requests before you and wait in expectation" (Psalm 5:3 NIV).

"May the words of my mouth and the meditation of my heart be pleasing in your sight, O Lord, my Rock and my Redeemer" (Psalm 19:14 NIV).

Praise God by quoting these Scriptures

Psalm 13:6 - I will sing to the Lord, for he has been good to me.

Psalm 52:9-53:1 - I will praise you forever for what you have done; in your name I will hope, for your name is good. I will praise you in the presence of your saints.

Psalm 18:2 - The Lord is my rock, my fortress and my deliverer; my God is my rock, in whom I take refuge. He is my shield and the horn of my salvation, my stronghold.

Psalm 57:10 - For great is your love, reaching to the heavens; your faithfulness reaches to the skies.

Psalm 59:16 - But I will sing of your strength, in the morning I will sing of your love; for you are my fortress, my refuge in times of trouble.

Psalm 63:1 - O God, you are my God; earnestly I seek you. My soul thirsts for you, my body longs for you in a dry and weary land where there is no water.

Psalm 63:4 - I will praise you as long as I live, and in your name I will lift up my hands.

Psalm 63:7 - Because you are my help, I sing in the shadow of your wings.

Psalm 19:1 - The heavens declare the glory of God; the skies proclaim the work of his hands.

Psalm 36:5 - Your love, O Lord, reaches to the heavens, your faithfulness to the skies.

Psalm 40:5 - Many, O Lord my God, are the wonders you have done. The things you planned for us no one can recount to you; were I to speak and tell of them, they would be too many to declare.

Recognize God's Intervention in Your Life

Psalm 18:6 - In my distress I called to the Lord; I cried to my God for help. From his temple he heard my voice; my cry came before him, into his ears.

Psalm 18:16 - He reached down from on high and took hold of me; he drew me out of deep waters.

Psalm 18:28 - You, O Lord, keep my lamp burning; my God turns my darkness into light.

Psalm 21:1 - O Lord, the king rejoices in your strength. How great is his joy in the victories you give!

Psalm 30:11-12 - You turned my wailing into dancing; you removed my sackcloth and clothed me with joy, that my heart may sing to you and not be silent. O Lord my God, I will give you thanks forever.

Thank God for the Blessings of Your Life

Psalm 3:5 - I lie down and sleep; I wake again, because the Lord sustains me.

Confess Your Sins

Psalm 51:4 - Against you, you only, have I sinned and done what is evil in your sight, so that you are proved right when you speak and justified when you judge.

Make Promises to God

Psalm 48:14 - For you God are our God for ever and ever; you will be our guide even to the end.

Psalm 56:3 - When I am afraid, I will trust in you.

Ask God to Lead You Each Day

Psalm 5:8 - Lead me, O Lord, in your righteousness because of my enemies--make straight your way before me.

Psalm 12:7 - O Lord, you will keep us safe and protect us from such people forever.

Psalm 25:4-5 - Show me your ways, O Lord, teach me your paths; guide me in your truth and teach me, for you are God my Savior, and my hope is in you all day long.

Psalm 25:20 - Guard my life and rescue me; let me not be put to shame, for I take refuge in you.

Psalm 27:11 - Teach me your way, O Lord; lead me in a straight path because of my oppressors.

Psalm 31:14-16 - But I trust in you, O Lord; I say, "You are my God." My times are in your hands; deliver me from my enemies and from those who pursue me. Let your face shine on your servant; save me in your unfailing love.

Psalm 41:4 - I said, "O Lord, have mercy on me; heal me, for I have sinned against you."

Psalm 44:26 - Rise up and help us; redeem us because of your unfailing love.

If your mind wanders or you feel unsure about what to pray, use God's words.

Other scriptures work for this technique as well. Use the prayers of Mary, David, Jeremiah, Isaac, and Moses to build your prayer life.

PRAY OUT LOUD

A technique to help you stay focused during your prayer time is to pray out loud. When you speak out loud, you are more likely to use full sentences. Speaking out loud helps express your thoughts and your petitions in full. Praying out loud allows you to keep focused on God.

Make an outline of your prayer in your notebook.

Monday

Lord I praise you for: Good health
  Safe travel
Lord I thank you for News of the new baby
  Opportunity to witness to my friend
  Extra time this morning
Lord I ask you for: Peace in financial difficulties
  Health of my daughter
  Direction for my church
  Blessings for my pastor

As I pray for each of these items aloud I check them off. Tomorrow my list will look different. This simple exercise of focus and praying out loud is a dramatic way to keep your mind from wandering to the activities of the day or to the chores to be done later.

PRAY IN TEXAN

When you pray, pray in Texan, or in Louisianian, Californian, or Pennsylvanian. In other words, use everyday language. Pray the words and phrases that are common to you. There is no need to use phrases and words that come from some prayer book you've seen or some grand ol' saint you have heard pray.

This is a conversation with God your Father. You need not address Him in some formal, unfamiliar way.

My friend Allen [14] was an adult before he heard about Jesus. Some friends invited him to join a men's softball team. Team members talked to him about Jesus the Savior and Allen became a Christian. This first time that I heard Allen pray out loud was one of my most memorable spiritual experiences. He started out, "Dear Father." Then there was silence as he tried to form his next sentence. He finally said, "We love you God. Thank you for Jesus. Help us. Amen."

That simple prayer, prayed in his halting speech pattern, was extraordinary. He expressed in those few words the fullness of the love he felt for God. I will never forget it.

Some months later, I heard Allen pray aloud again. By then, he had learned all the phrases. He'd learned his "thees and thous." Now he knew exactly what to say. This time he didn't stammer or stumble. Sadly, his prayer now sounded rote, stale, and dry.

Don't let this happen to you. In your quiet time, strive to talk to God as if he is your best friend sitting right next to you. Because He is. God does not want to hear a perfect, poetic phrase when we pray. He wants to hear words and thoughts directly from our hearts.

Talk to God in your normal words. Avoid phrase repetitions unless they truly express your feelings.

To rediscover the innocence of prayer may take a lot of effort on your part. Listen closely to yourself when you pray. Do you use the word "Father" in every sentence? Do you overuse the word "just"? What other words or phrases do you use only in prayer? Maybe you should get rid of these words. As you recognize these words and phrases, evaluate them. Would other words and phrases sound more natural? What do you say in conversations with friends? Use those same kinds of words in your prayers.

Jesus said not to use vain repetitions when praying. He was asking us to use our regular language in His presence. One person I regularly hear pray aloud uses the word "father" in every sentence of his prayer. It seems to be a nervous habit of which I am sure he is unaware. When a habit like that develops in our prayers, it detracts from our ability to communicate with God.

So pull out your Texas drawl or your New York accent or your thick brogue and speak to God as you would to your best friend.

Practice writing a prayer, which uses only your everyday language and does not contain any "religious" words or phrases. Ask God to help you learn to pray spontaneously and freely in all your prayers.

SIGN LANGUAGE

Sign language is not only a useful and practical tool; it is also a beautiful expression of the meaning, depth, and intensity of words.

I'm not a sign language expert but I have devised a few signs that depict words for me. Some of these I have picked up from watching interpreters and some are signs I invented. My personal sign language helps me express my love to God.

When I seem unable to find words to express what I feel, I can usually make up a hand motion to express my feelings.

For example, if I am overwhelmed with love for Jesus, I can express it through sign language as follows:

I ------------Point to myself
Love-------Wrap arms around my shoulders
You--------Point to Heaven

I know it is simplistic and rudimentary, but it works for me. Expressing myself in sign language helps me worship God when I don't know what to say. Here are some ideas to get you started with your own personal sign language.

God, You-----------Point to Heaven
are awesome!-------Clap hands together, applause

Or

You-----------------Point to Heaven
give me--------------Hands out, palms up (as if to receive)
joy--------------------Hands up, fingers outstretched in an
                                upward motion

Or

You-------------------Point to Heaven
are merciful---------Move hands together up and
                                down like a wave

Or

You-------------------Point to Heaven
are peace-------------Fold hands under side of
                                face as if asleep

Using your personal sign language is simple yet profound. Use it to express praise or pleading. For some of us, using our hands and arms in prayer is easy because we talk with our hands anyway. But if making up your own signs overwhelms you, purchase a sign language handbook that contains photographs of sign language motions.

Expressing your feelings with sweeping motions of your arms or with finger movements fills your worship with joy and freshness.

Write out phrases that you want to say in sign language. Draw reminders of the motions you have designed. Refer to these drawings when you pray.

PRAYING IN SECTIONS

Make a prayer notebook and divide it into three equal sections. Label each one as follows: praise, thanksgiving, and petition.

Praise

In the first section, make a list of the attributes of God (holy, powerful, omnipotent, creative, healer, compassionate, merciful, etc.). Use this section to begin your prayer. Repeat the words listed and tell God you love Him for who He is. For example, pray, "I love you, Lord, because you are the creator of the earth," or "I worship you, God, because you are holy and worthy of praise," or "I praise you for your power."

Thanksgiving

Use the second section to write down how you love God for all He has done. Make a list of blessings you are thankful for. Your list may include family, home, job, and church. Don't forget to list some unusual things in this list like good shoes, sunshine, red bud trees, etc. As you pray through this section, speak to God of the blessings He has given.

I received a copy of the book "10,000 Things to Praise God For." I was amazed to read nearly 500 pages of lists of things God has done. Listed in the book is everything from a child's hug to tape dispensers and from jelly beans to seatbelts. Your list can be just as amazing if you will look around to recognize all the things God has done for you.

Petition

In the third section, make a list of your needs and desires. To keep this from becoming long and unmanageable, divide the section into categories and put the categories into days of the week.

Monday	Family needs
Tuesday	Myself
Wednesday	The people I come in contact with daily
Thursday	Neighbors, neighborhood, and church
Friday	Nation and Elected officials
Saturday	Missionaries

Praying in three sections helps you remember that prayer is not only petition but praise and thanksgiving as well.

SOMETIMES, PRAY WITHOUT ASKING FOR ANYTHING

All too often our prayers are nothing but requests instead of an intimate time of love and worship. If we only come to Him asking for stuff, we restrict our ability to form an intimacy with Him, because we tend to base our relationship on what we get from Him. Sometimes we tend to think of God as our personal Santa Claus.

One technique you can use to overcome this difficulty is to pray an entire prayer without asking for anything.

You will have to work at this discipline. For a refreshing change in your prayer life, try to spend ten minutes talking to the Lord without any petition.

Make a list so you can pray without petition.

SOMETIMES, PRAY WITHOUT USING THE WORD 'BLESS'

A fresh approach to prayer is to pray a whole prayer and never use the word "bless." It is a hard task to accomplish because we have learned to repeat the word "bless" in our prayers. The word becomes a cliché. The solution is to find other words to use. Instead of saying, "Lord, bless my pastor," say, "Lord, give my pastor extra time for you today," or "Lord, show my pastor a new and special insight in the Word today." Or perhaps, "Lord, give him success in counseling today."

When you pray for a missionary, instead of using the one cover-all word "bless," pray specifically that the missionary will lead a person to Christ today. Ask God to encourage the missionary with a special Bible verse. Pray that the missionary will receive a special letter of encouragement from home today. Praying specifically gives you the opportunity to see the answers to your prayers.

Make a list of at least six names. Beside each name write a substitute for the word "bless" as you pray for that person.

SOMETIMES, PRAY AND USE THE WORD 'BLESS' IN A NEW WAY

I'm not prejudiced against blessing or using the word "bless." It can be a wonderful prayer tool if used well. Sometimes, try this prayer technique with the word "bless." Ask God to bless someone and mean it in a new and definitive way. We can learn to fully express what we mean when we say "bless" as in this prayer: "Lord, bless Edith. Just bless her so much that she is overwhelmed by your presence, love, and abundance." Ask God to make Himself known to your friend just this moment while you are praying. Then check on the person later and see how God answered your prayer.

List as many people as you can that you would like for God to bless. Pray through your list periodically during your quiet time.

MAKE A PRAYER JOURNAL

Begin to train yourself to pray more specifically by writing your prayers. Build a prayer journal section consisting of blank pages. As you put your prayers in writing, use full sentences and sub-headings. The freedom to write out prayers long or short allows you to follow the Lord's leading each day.

When you take time to listen to God while praying, He may reveal new insights to you that you will also want to record. Use a different color pen to record verses and further thoughts that come to your mind as you listen to God in your prayer time. Even your praises can be expanded as you learn to write your prayers.

PRAY FOR YOUR KIDS

For many years I have prayed Psalm 20 for my daughter. She is a beautiful, bright, and ambitious young woman. Confident, capable, and successful, she loves the Lord and lives her life serving Him. Yet I know she experiences some doubts and other emotions in her daily life. She usually tries to hide these from everyone, but God has given me, as her mother, special insights into her heart. So I pray Psalm 20 for her like this:

> Verse 1 states, "May the Lord answer you when you are in distress; may the name of the God of Jacob protect you."

> I pray: **Father, when Cherry's life is in turmoil and it seems to be too much for her to handle, I ask you to protect her.**

> Verse 2: "May he send you help from the sanctuary and grant you support from Zion."

I pray: **Father, only you can send help and support to her. Her relationship with you is the springboard for your action in her life. Please support her today.**

Verse 3: "May he remember all your sacrifices and accept your burnt offerings."

I pray: **Father, as you regard her, remember what a good girl she has always been. Recall her service to you and let her good record be the guide in how you deal with her. Shower her with your blessings because of her Christian life, generous spirit, and love for you.**

Verse 4: "May he give you the desire of your heart and make all your plans succeed."

I pray: **Father, bless Cherry with fulfillment of her desires. Make her successful in all her efforts.**

Verse 5: "We will shout for joy when you are victorious and will lift up our banners in the name of our God. May the Lord grant all your requests."

I pray: **Father, as Cherry wins victories, we will bless, honor, and give the glory to you. Father, I ask you to grant her requests.**

As I have watched our daughter receive honors, have successes in life and serve God, I praise God for His answer to my prayers in Psalm 20.

******

Most of his life, I have prayed Psalm 72 for my son. He is the one in our family who plans ahead. In fact, he drives us all crazy with his advance organization. He is apt to ask what time we will leave on a trip eight months in advance. He is a man of progress and leadership. David prayed Psalm 72 for his son Solomon. Here is how I use Psalm 72 to help me pray for my boy.

Verse 1: "Endow the king of your justice, O God, the royal son with your righteousness."

I pray: **Lord, give Brett a heart of justice and righteousness. Cause him to recognize right and wrong and to follow right.**

Verse 2: "He will judge your people in righteousness, your afflicted ones with justice."

I pray: **Give him the ability to recognize righteousness in others and to be a person who helps bring out the good in others. Give him discernment when choosing friends.**

Verses 3 and 4: "The mountains will bring prosperity to the people, the hills the fruit of righteousness. He will defend the afflicted among the people and save the children of the needy."

I pray: **Father, let Brett be the one to stand up for the rights of those who are down and out. Give him compassion for kids who need to know you. Cause him to reach out to people even if no else does.**

Verse 5: "He will endure as long as the sun, as long as the moon, through all generations."

I pray: **Give Brett stability and strength. May he be a blessing to young and old alike.**

Verses 6 and 7: "He will be like rain falling on a mown field, like showers watering the earth. In his days the righteous will flourish; propriety will abound till the moon is no more."

I pray: **Help Brett to be winsome and likeable so that he can lead people to you and your salvation. Give him strength to work long hours.**

Verse 8: "He will rule from sea to sea and from river to the ends of the earth."

I pray: **Give him a ministry that will make a difference to a lost world.**

Verse 13: "He will take pity on the weak and needy and save the needy from death."

I pray: **Lord, make Brett a person who will rescue the hurting and care about needy people.**

Verse 15: "Long may he live! May gold from Sheba be given him. May people ever pray for him and bless him all day long."

I pray: **Bless him with health and healthy living. May the people touched by his ministry help and support him. May they pray for him and bless him.**

I wasn't sure why I was praying verse 15 when he was young, but after he gave his life to the ministry and moved to the mission field to plant a church, I understood how God would use other godly people in his life and ministry. I had been praying for these people all along through verse 15.

You can see how using these Psalms fits the personalities of my children. Since I now have a daughter-in-law and a son-in-law and grandchildren, I am searching for specific passages of Scripture that fit their personalities and needs so that I can pray God's own words over them.

As you read scripture during your quiet time, look for verses and groups of verses that can become your prayers for your family members.

PRAY FOR YOURSELF

I love to pray Psalm 18 for myself. It requires almost no changes to the text to personalize this wonderful Psalm.

- I love you, O Lord, my strength.
- The Lord is my rock, my fortress, and my deliverer; my God is my rock, in whom I take refuge. Lord, you are my shield and the horn of my salvation, my stronghold.
- I call to you, Lord. You are worthy of praise. You save me from my enemies.
- The cords of death entangled me; the torrents of destruction overwhelmed me.
- The cords of the grave coiled around me; the snares of death confronted me.
- In my distress I call to you, Lord; I cried to you for help. From your temple, you heard my voice; my cry came before you, into your ears.
- You reached down from on high and took hold of me; you drew me out of deep waters.

- You rescued me from my powerful enemy, from my foes, who were too strong for me.
- They confronted me in the day of my disaster, but you, Lord, are my support.
- You brought me out into a spacious place; you rescued me because you delighted in me.
- You, O Lord, keep my lamp burning; you turn my darkness into light.
- With your help I can advance against a troop; with you I can scale a wall.
- As for you, God, your way is perfect; the word of the Lord is flawless. You are a shield for all who take refuge in you.

Even now as I read verse 16, my heart leaps to my throat. I am so grateful to the Lord for His mercy. Even though He is God, He reached down and took hold of me and pulled me from the pit.

Verse 19 always puts my heart on shouting ground too. When I was a young girl, my family took a vacation to South Texas. One day we crossed the border into Mexico on a shopping trip. While we were there, we began to feel claustrophobic as we became aware of the narrow streets, the masses of people, and the bumper-to-bumper traffic. When we returned across the border in the afternoon and pulled our car onto the wide superhighway in Texas, we all had the same feeling of moving into a spacious place. Later when I read verse 19, I remembered that feeling of relief as we came home that day and I realize how God has not only saved me, but He has rescued me and put me in a spacious place.

If you have difficulty with personalizing Scripture with this prayer technique, try reading a modern language version of the Bible such as the New Century Version or The Message. Sometimes, these modern translations will use fresh words and phrases that stimulate your creative juices enough to get started.

What a blessing to be able to turn to Psalm 20 and pray God's words for my daughter or Psalm 72 and pray God's words over my son. As a parent, it is often hard to know what to pray for our children. From our children's beginning days, we feel frustrated about their sleeping and eating routines.

When they are children, we watch them develop and we wonder how to pray. When they reach their teenage years, we begin to allow them to make decisions and we hold our breath. Even in their adult years, we want to see their lives happy and fruitful in God's service.

It is so difficult to know how to pray. Praying scripture over your child through all the stages of life will help you to stay in touch with God's will for them no matter what is happening in their lives.

PRAY FOR YOUR SPOUSE

How do you pray for your husband or wife? Ask God to give him/her a friend. Someone to play racquetball or golf with. Someone to shop with. Someone who is like him/her. Someone who has integrity. Someone who has strong morals. Someone who will challenge your spouse when he or she is wrong. Someone who will encourage, push in the right directions, and be a calming influence.

One of the greatest assets to your marriage can be a godly, faithful friend for your spouse.

In your prayer notebook, set aside a section for prayers for your spouse. Pray for his/her health. Ask God to bless your spouse.

ACCEPT THE SILENCE

My friend Millie[15] was going through the breakup of her marriage and she was watching her family fall apart before her eyes. She spent hours and hours in prayer and Bible study trying to find peace in the situation. She found a lot of comfort in scripture and clung to promises from God's Word to hold her life together during this time. One day she called me.

She had been reading Oswald Chambers' devotional book "My Utmost for His Highest" and the words she found there touched her deeply. She read them to me, "Can God trust you with the silence?"

My friend had felt the silence profoundly as her life crumbled before her. She had begged God night after night for a sign that everything would be okay in her life. It seemed as if God was not hearing her and was not speaking to her either. The words of Oswald Chambers caused her to realize that God would work in His time and at His pace. She also realized that her faith in God would be tested during times of silence. Would she trust God?

Those profound words from Oswald Chambers have gripped my heart too. I am an action-oriented person. Put a problem before me and I'll make a list of the three steps needed to solve the problem. Call me to discuss a situation and I'll end the conversation with a "to do" list for us both.

This is my nature. It sometimes leaves me thoroughly frustrated in my relationship with God because sometimes He is silent. It has been difficult to learn to wait on His answer and accept the silence. But that Chambers statement has helped me tremendously. "Can God trust me with silence?"

During my prayer time, there will be moments of complete silence when He doesn't speak. There may also be days, weeks, and even years when I cannot write a prayer answer in my prayer journal. Do I continue to trust God anyway? There may be times when I have nothing to cling to except His Word. If so, do I love, worship, and trust Him anyway? Can God trust you and me with silence?

To experience a devil-defeating, heart-comforting, soul-awakening, life-changing quiet time, develop a love for the silences. Not only does God ask us to accept the silence but to love the opportunity to trust Him.

List what God has been silent about. Beside each line write the words, "I trust God with this silence."

In her novel "Vienna Prelude," Bodie Thoene's character Elisa speaks to God in her music. As she plays the violin, the music becomes her prayer to God. Listen to her words:

> This is me, God! Elisa. I once saw you in all the world. But the world is dark now, Lord. Full. Full of darkness. Close your eyes for a moment God, and let me sing to you. Let me remember that you are here. Here in the notes. Smiling down as I play for you. Just this moment, God, let me sing to you. And maybe in the song, I will forget whether I am singing to you or you are singing to me.

I challenge you to spend one hour with the Lord on your knees. Look at your clock, and do not get up from your knees until one hour has passed. It will be tough. You will have to be determined to do it, but please try it.

Let God speak to you during that hour. Let the silences happen. You will have to fight to keep your mind from wandering, but if you will listen, you will hear His gentle whisper, and God will give you direction for your life. His direction will be specific. His words will be encouraging. And, like Elisa, you may forget whether you are speaking to Him or He is speaking to you.

DON'T GET DISCOURAGED

In the book "The Proverbs 31 Lady and Other Impossible Dreams" the author writes about the original liberated woman—the Proverbs 31 lady. She was the perfect housewife, mother, wife, and entrepreneur. When the author tried to imitate the Proverbs 31 lady, she discovered that the more she tried and failed, the more she became like the lady in the verses through the power of Christ.

The same is true for prayer. I know from experience that the more you try to meet God daily and grow spiritually in daily doses, you will often feel like a failure. But in the failing you will become more intimate and closer to God.

About Karen Porter

Author/Speaker

Karen Porter is an international retreat and seminar speaker and a successful businesswoman. She is the author of six books including *If You Give a Girl A Giant,* and *I'll Bring the Chocolate* and *Speak Like Jesus.*

Business/Professional

Karen served as Vice President of International Marketing of a major food company in Texas for more than 30 years. She traveled around the world and her varied experiences (including dinners with Fidel Castro) contribute to the richness and depth of her writing and speaking.

Karen and her husband George are the owners of **Bold Vision Books**, an independent, Christian publishing company. Learn more about publishing opportunities at **www.boldvisionbooks.com**.

Trainer/Mentoring Ministry

Karen served on the Board of Directions and national teaching staff of **CLASSEMINARS, Inc.**, the nation's premier trainer of Christian leaders and speakers. She also serves as president of the board of **AWSA: Advanced Writers Speakers Association** and served as chairman of **the Board of Directors of First Place for Health**, one of the nation's top health and nutrition programs.

Karen coaches aspiring writers and speakers to excel in the techniques, craft, and business, as well as the heart, of speaking and writing.

Personal

Karen says her marriage to George is her greatest achievement, but she'd love to talk to you about her five grandchildren! In her spare time, Karen continues her life-long quest to find the perfect purse.

Karen is a people person, plain and simple and you will love to laugh with her and maybe even cry a little as she shares her joys and struggles.

Bold Vision Books
PO BOX 2011
Friendswood, Texas 77549

www.boldvisionbooks.com

 Connect with Karen on Facebook

and Twitter.

Invite Karen Porter to your next event.
www.karenporter.com
Email: kaeporter@gmail.com

References:

1 Michael Yaconelli, Messy Spirituality, Zondervan, 2007, page 115

2 Author Unknown

3 Author Unknown

4 Volumes have been written on the merits of various translations. Check them out in your local Christian bookstore.

5 This list of Bible translations/versions/paraphrases is not meant to be exhaustive or in-depth. The descriptions are the author's opinion.

6 Answer: Who may dwell and who may live?
7 Answer: The Lord
8 Answer: Walking, Doing, Speaking
9 Answer: No slander, No wrong, no Slur
10 Answer: Truth, Compassion, Confidence
11 Answer: Therefore, Since
12 2 Corinthians 4:7, NIV
13 Not the person's real name
14 Not the person's real name
15 Not the person's real name

www.ingramcontent.com/pod-product-compliance
Lightning Source LLC
LaVergne TN
LVHW021350080426
835508LV00020B/2198